BEHAVIORAL INERTIA APPROACH TO MODELLING STOCK PRICES

N. LALITHA

ACKNOWLEDGEMENTS

I would like to express my sincere thanks to Professor D. N. Rao for his constant encouragement, advice and expert guidance. I have gained immensely from him during the initiation, progress and completion of this study. I am particularly thankful to his patient hearing of my ideas and his appreciation and constructive criticism of the same. I will always cherish this period.

I would also like to thank all the faculty members and the administrative staff of the Centre for Economic Studies and Planning, Jawaharlal Nehru University for their support.

My sincere thanks go to Dr. (Mrs.) S. K. Jolly, Principal Shyama Prasad Mukherji College (for women), University of Delhi, for her support.

I am thankful to my sister N. Sangeeta for her colossal help during various stages of the study.

This work would not have taken its final shape without the support from my family.

CONTENTS **Pages**

CHAPTER 4   76

BEHAVIORAL PRINCIPLES OF STOCK MARKET

LIST OF TABLES

GLOSSARY OF ABBREVIATIONS

AARs	Average Monthly Abnormal Returns
ADF test	Augmented Dickey Fuller Test
ADRs	American Depository Receipts
AMEX	The American Stock Exchange
APT	Arbitrage Pricing Theory
AR coefficients	Autoregressive coefficients
ARCH	Autoregressive Conditional Heteroskedasticity
BC Intervals	Bias Corrected Confidence Intervals
BCa	Accelerated Bias Corrected Confidence Intervals
BE/ME	Ratio of Book Value of Common Equity to Market Value of Equity
BHARs	Buy and Hold Abnormal Returns
BHBEME	Big and High BE/ME Portfolio
BHBEME WTD	Big and High BE/ME Value Wtd Portfolio
BHEPS	Big and High EPS/P Portfolio
BHEPS WTD	Big and High EPS/P Value Wtd Portfolio
BLBEME	Big and Low BE/ME Portfolio
BLBEME WTD	Big and Low BE/ME Value Wtd Portfolio
BLEPS	Big and Low EPS/P Portfolio
BLEPS WTD	Big and Low EPS/P Value Wtd Portfolio
	BLU estimators Best Linear Unbiased estimators
BMBEME	Big and Medium BE/ME Portfolio
BMBEME WTD	Big and Medium BE/ME Value Wtd Portfolio
BMEPS	Big and Medium EPS/P Portfolio
BMEPS WTD	Big and Medium EPS/P Value Wtd Portfolio
BOD	Board of Directors

BOE	Board of Executives
BOISL	Bank of Shareholding Limited
BPT	Behavioral Portfolio Theory
BSE	Bombay Stock Exchange
BSV	Barberis, Shleifer and Vishny
C/P	Ratio of Cash Flow per Share to Price of the Stock
CAPM	Capital Asset Pricing Model
CARs	Cumulative Average Monthly Abnormal Returns
CCAPM	Consumption CAPM
CDF	Cumulative Distribution Functions
CDSL	Central Depository Services Limited
CEO	Chief Executive Officer
CRSP	Center for Research in Security Prices
CVF	Critical Value Function
DBS	Double Bootstrap
DCA	Department of Company Affairs
DEA	Department of Economic Affairs
DGP	Data Generating Process
DHS	Daniel, Hirshleifer and Subrahmanyam
DIP	Disclosures and Investor Protection
DW statistic	Durbin-Watson Statistic
EDF	Empirical Distribution Function
EMH	Efficient Market Hypothesis
EPS/P	Ratio of Earnings per Share to the Price of Stock
ERP	Error in Rejection Probability
FDB	Fast Double Bootstrap
FII	Foreign Institutional Investors
GARCH	Generalized ARCH

GDP	Gross Domestic Product
GDRs	Global Depository Receipts
GS	Growth Rate of Sales
HBEME	High BE/ME Portfolio
HBEME WTD	High BE/ME Value Wtd Portfolio
HEPSP	High EPS/P Portfolio
HEPSP WTD	High EPS/P Value Wtd Portfolio
HML	Difference Between the Return on a Portfolio of High BE/ME Stocks and the Return on a Portfolio of Low BE/ME Stocks
HWZ	Hein, Westfall and Zhang
i.i.d.	Independent and Identically Distributed
ICAPM	Intertemporal CAPM
ICICI	Industrial Credit and Investment Corporation of India Limited
IDBI	Industrial Development Bank of India Limited
IEPF	Investor Education and Protection Fund
IPO	Initial Public Offerings
IT	Information Technology
LBEME	Low BE/ME Portfolio
LBEME WTD	Low BE/ME Value Wtd Portfolio
LEPSP	Low EPS/P Portfolio
LEPSP WTD	Low EPS/P Value Wtd Portfolio
LM test	Lagrangian multiplier test
LR test	Likelihood Ratio Test
LSE	The London Stock Exchange
LSV	Lakonishok, Shleifer and Vishny
MBEME	Medium BE/ME Portfolio
MBEME WTD	Medium BE/ME Value Wtd Portfolio
MEPSP	Medium EPS/P Portfolio

MEPSP WTD	Medium EPS/P Value Wtd Portfolio
MF	Mutual funds
MMV	Multifactor Minimum Variance
Nasdaq	National Association of Securities Dealers Automated Quotations
NAV	Net Asset Value
NCAER	National Council of Applied Economic Research
NIM	New Issue Market
NPV	Net Present Value
NSCCL	The National Clearing Corporation of India Limited
NSDL	National Securities Depository Limited
NSE.	National Stock Exchange
NTPC	National Thermal Power Corporation Limited
NYSE	New York Stock Exchange
OLS	Ordinary Least Square
ONGC	Oil and Natural Gas Corporation Limited
OTC market	Over-the-Counter Market
RPF	Rejection Probability Function
SBTS	Screen Based Trading System
SEBI	Securities and Exchange Board of India
SGF	Settlement Guarantee Fund
SHBEME	Small and High BE/ME Portfolio
SHBEME WTD	Small and High BE/ME Value Wtd Portfolio
SHEPS	Small and High EPS/P Portfolio
SHEPS WTD	Small and High EPS/P Value Wtd Portfolio
SLBEME	Small and Low BE/ME Portfolio
SLBEME WTD	Small and Low BE/ME Value Wtd Portfolio
SLEPS	Small and Low EPS/P Portfolio
SLEPS WTD	Small and Low EPS/P Value Wtd Portfolio

SMB	Difference Between thè Return on a Portfolio of Small Stocks and the Return on a Portfolio of Large Stocks
SMBEME	Small and Medium BE/ME Portfolio
SMBEME WTD	Small and Medium BE/ME Value Wtd Portfolio
SMEPS	Small and Medium EPS/P Portfolio
SMEPS WTD	Small and Medium EPS/P Value Wtd Portfolio
TCS	Tata Consultancy Services Limited
TMT	Technology, Media and Telecom
TSE	Tokyo Stock Exchange
UIN	Unique Identification Number
VLIT	Value as a Long Term Investment

CHAPTER 1: INTRODUCTION

Reforms in the stock market form one of the major success stories of the Indian economic reforms. The Indian stock market has gained a position of prominence both in terms of number of companies listed and in terms of market capitalization. The breadth of the Indian market is increasing rapidly. This can be seen by the fact that the number of companies with a \$15 billion plus market capitalization has more than tripled from 2001. Similarly, in the \$1-5 billion market capitalization bracket, the number has more than doubled over the same period. Indeed the listing of large-capitalization companies like Oil and Natural Gas Corporation Ltd (ONGC), Tata Consultancy Services Ltd (TCS) and National Thermal Power Corporation Ltd (NTPC) is increasing the breadth of the market thereby making the market more attractive for the large and long-term investors.

While India's investors population has remained stuck at two crores for over a decade, indications are that the number of investors entering the stock market will go up in the coming years. Returns on various savings instruments like bank deposits, post office deposits have fallen in the present low interest regime, making investment in stock markets worthwhile. Pension funds are also expected to enter the markets soon. The new generation of enterprising and dynamic youth is expected to be less risk averse than its earlier generation and have greater participation in the stock market.

Foreign investors find the stability and growth of Indian market vis-à-vis other emerging markets as a major incentive to invest in stocks of Indian companies. The good performance of the corporate sector along with satisfactory economy level indicators predicts an upward rising long-term trend for the market despite the rise being punctuated by short term volatility.

1.1 OBJECTIVE OF THE STUDY

One aspect of the market that is of great interest to all participants in the stock market is the stock price formation. It is now widely recognized that Sharpe (1964) and Lintner (1965) and Mossin's (1966) Capital Asset Pricing Model (CAPM) and its other variants have little practical use. Most markets are dominated by stocks which show little covariance with the market index and whose returns can therefore be predicted only by looking at firm and industry specific factors. The hype associated with all sorts of dot.com companies and media companies that pushed stock markets worldwide during the later part of nineties and early two thousand poses an interesting question as to whether such boom in technology and media stocks was justified by fundamentals or was it a mere fad? Using the behavioral inertia approach, the present study tries to show that the market was indeed driven by the craze surrounding such stocks.

In general, pricing models are used as a benchmark to determine the expected rate of return on an asset. This expected rate of return is then used as the discounting factor in a valuation model to determine price as the Net Present Value (NPV) of future stream of dividends. In this set up therefore, price is treated as an outcome of a two-step estimation process with expected rate of return estimated in the first step and price in the second step.

A very popular returns generation model is the Fama & French three-factor model. We fit a Fama and French model to the portfolios obtained by grouping sample stocks on the basis of various criteria of ranking. A joint test of all portfolios for each criterian is done in a multivariate framework to study the cross section of returns across portfolios.

Instead of the above mentioned two-step approach we propose a single step determination of price formation. Our approach differs from the usual approach of modeling stock price behavior in the following regards:

(1) Unlike conventional estimation procedures based on optimizing principles, which makes huge demand on investors' knowledge, our approach is less information intensive.

In an uncertain world, individuals treat only direct experience as containing genuine information. On the basis of past experiences they derive inferences and therefore display inertia or habit persistence. Inertia is incorporated in the model by using lagged dependent variables. Apart from past prices individuals use various indicators (both firm level and economy level) in guessing future prices. How this information is incorporated in price formation varies across individuals. Such random behavior by individuals creates uncertainity and caprice. The uncertainity element is captured by the random error term. Caprice is also modeled as exhibiting inertia. So the current price is defined as a function of lagged prices and firm level variables and beta which measures the sensitivity of the stocks to movements in the market.

(2) Unlike the usual approach of choosing the model by looking at its fit on the sample data, our model is an outcome of an explicit theory of economic behavior and change. This has important implications for drawing inferences. A poor performance of the model observed either as misspecified errors or coefficients with wrong signs is treated as evidence against the theory. Again, as against the conventional method of adjusting the model, in our approach we reformulate the hypothesis regarding economic behavior by looking at the source of the problem.

(3) Ours is a simple approach that allows for biases in individual behavior and treats them as incompletely rational. Therefore, our approach does not entail calculations of rationally expected returns, which in any case cannot be calculated in ex ante terms.

(4) Following another behavior principle that investors seek comfort in familiarity and therefore do not hold a diversified portfolio, which would nullify industry associated risk, we estimated the model at the stock level.

(5) The use of the technique of bootstrap in the study of Indian market is another distinct feature of the study. Though the model is consistently estimated by Ordinary Least Square (OLS), the presence of lagged dependent variables questions the unbiasedness of the OLS estimates. So we undertook a bootstrap estimation which gave us empirical refinements over using an asymptotic first order theory. The technique of recursive bootstrap is developed and used to test not only the model but also the Breusch-Godfrey higher order serial correlation diagnostic test.

1.2 CHAPTER SCHEME

This study is divided into six chapters and some appendices. This introductory chapter is followed by an outline of the growth of Indian stock market. A brief growth profile of U.S, U.K and Japanese stock market is also outlined. In the next chapter we discuss the various asset pricing models that are used in empirical work. The shortcomings of many popular models are also noted. This chapter evaluates the Fama and French model both theoretically and empirically.

In the next chapter we focus on the behavioral principles guiding an individual's behavior. Here we discuss the various biases that individuals are prone to. A behavioral model for describing stock price behavior is developed and its empirical testing is undertaken.

In Chapter 5 we elaborate on the technique of bootstrap. The econometric refinements associated with it are highlighted. A brief survey of the literature that reports the use of bootstrap is also done. We also report the results of bootstrapping the serial correlation LM test, and wald statistic for the test of inertia. Finally summary and conclusions of the study are given in chapter 6.

CHAPTER 2: STOCK MARKETS IN INDIA: A PERSPECTIVE

In this chapter we trace the growth of Indian stock markets since its inception and note the measures that have improved its functioning. **Section 2.1** highlights the growth in the Indian capital market by looking at some statistics pertaining to the number of investors, market capitalization, trading volumes and turn-over ratios. In today's globalized world, investors can reduce their risk exposure by holding cross-country stocks in their portfolios. The increased role of Foreign Institutional Investors (FII), in the Indian market and the position of the Indian stock market in the securities market of the world is also noted in this section. **Section 2.2** gives a brief discussion of the growth profiles of the USA, UK and the Japanese Stock Exchanges. In **Section 2.3** we look at the growth of Indian stock exchanges from 1830 onwards. Establishment of Bombay Stock Exchange (BSE) in 1887, and National Stock Exchange (NSE) in 1992 are the milestones in the history of Indian capital market. In this section we also note the establishment of the Securities and Exchange Board of India (SEBI) and its role as the market watchdog. In **Section 2.4** we list some of the reform measures undertaken in the recent past. Finally, we note down the areas which still call for some changes to further improve the functioning of the Indian stock market in **Section 2.5**.

2.1 GROWTH IN THE CAPITAL MARKET

The process of liberalization and privatization started in the nineties increased the role of the private corporate sector in the Indian industrialization process. This growth of the corporate sector has been made possible due to the increased availability of savings. While the short-term funds come from banks, medium-term or long-term funds are either raised from the capital market or are borrowed from the long-term lending institutions like IDBI, ICICI etc. A sharp rise in the level of paid up capital is indicative of the increasing reliance of the corporate sector on the external source of finance. The share of capital market based instruments in resources raised externally, which was quite significant in the nineties, declined from 2001-02 onwards. This decline was due to the lack-luster performance of the secondary market. Of the two segments of the capital market, namely the primary market and the secondary market, it is the former in which the new capital is raised by the companies. The New Issue Market (NIM) or the primary market is thus very important from the point of economic growth. The secondary market on the other hand, is the market for old or already issued securities. The secondary market is composed of the exchange traded market and the OTC market. The OTC markets are informal markets where trades are negotiated and it covers most of the trade in government securities. The secondary market serves the important task of providing liquidity by enabling investors adjust their portfolio in response to changes in their assessment of risks and returns. By imparting liquidity and price stability to the securities it helps companies raise additional capital in the 'NIM' with greater ease. Thus, both the segments of the capital market are equally important from the point of view of supply of capital to the companies.

Over the years and particularly in the recent past, the capital market has contributed significantly to corporate growth (and economic development) not only in term of the quantum of funds but also in terms of the nature of funds provided to the corporate sector. The supply of funds to the capital market comes from individual savers, corporate savings, insurance companies, banks and other financial intermediaries. SEBI in association with National Council of Applied Economic Research (NCAER) conducted a survey of investors in 1998-99 and then followed it up in 2000-01. The survey estimated that a total of 13.1 million or 7.4% of all Indian households totaling 21 million individuals directly invested in equity shares or debentures or both during 2000-01. Though the percentage of investor households is very small the spurt in investors' interest acquires great significance when compared with the investor base of just about a million share holders in 1970. The survey also found that the number of debenture owning households and individual debenture holders far exceeds household and individual equity investors. Of the total 13.1 million investor households, 9.6 million households owned bonds or debentures, whereas only 6.5 million investor households owned equity shares. Further the percentage of households investing in equity or debentures is more in urban areas than in rural areas. This difference is more in case of equities compared to debentures.

The average annual capital mobilization from the primary market has grown manifold since the last two-three decades. It received a further boost during the first half of the nineties with the capital raised by non-governmental public companies rising sharply from Rupees 43,120 million in 1990-91 to Rupees 264,170 million in 1994-95. Thereafter, there has been a decline due to conditions prevailing in the secondary market. However, the year 2003-04 took a turn around in its performance as compared to the previous year by mobilizing Rupees 32,100 million. The capital raised, which used to be less than 1% of gross domestic savings in the 1970s, increased to about 13% in the 1992-93 but thereafter declined. Though there has been a considerable increase in the amount mobilized in 2003-04, when seen as a percentage of the gross domestic savings, it is a low 1.2%. Private placements which are the preferred form of raising resources accounted for 89% of total resources mobilized through domestic issues by corporate sector during 2003-04.

There are 23 exchanges in the country which offer screen based trading system, with NSE and BSE being the dominant players. All the exchanges follow a systematic settlement period. All the trades taking place over a trading cycle (day = T) are settled together on day T+2. There were 9368 trading members registered with SEBI at the end of March 2004.

The market capitalization has grown over the period indicating more companies using the trading platform of the stock exchange. The all India market capitalization is estimated at Rupees 13,187,953 million at the end of March 2004. The market capitalization ratio defined as the value of listed stocks divided by GDP increased sharply to 52.3% in 2003-04 against 28.5% in the previous year indicating a growth in the stock market size.

The trading volumes on exchanges have been witnessing phenomenal growth over the past decade. The trading volume which peaked at Rupees 28,809,900 million in 2000-01, fell substantially to Rupees 9,689,093 million in 2003-04. However the year 2003-04 notched an increase in trading volume to the tune of Rupees 16,204,977 million. The turnover ratio, which reflects the volume of trading in relation to the size of the market has been increasing by leaps and bounds after the advent of screen based trading system by the NSE. The turnover ratio for the year 2003-04 was 122.9%. Most of the increase in turnover took place at the big exchanges. The NSE remained the market leader with more than 85% of total turnover (volumes on all segments) in 2003-04. The top five stock exchanges accounted for 99.88% of turnover and the rest 18 exchanges for less than 0.12% during 2003-04. About 10 exchanges reported nil trading volume during the year.

Along with the growth of the market there has been a change in the composition of investors over time. Foreign Institutional Investors (FII) with their financial might are increasingly registering their presence in the Indian stock market. Their increased prominence can be seen from the increase in the number of FIIs registered with SEBI. Institutional investors have also strengthened their position. Mutual funds (MF) have emerged as a safe investment vehicle for participating in the stock market. During the last decade the resources mobilized by mutual funds have increased from Rupees 112,440 million in 1993-94 to Rupees 476,840 million in 2003-04. This performance by MFs is the outcome of evolution of a regulatory framework for MFs, tax concessions offered by government and preference of investors for passive investing.

The Indian economy is getting integrated with the global market, though in a limited way, through Euro issues. Since they were permitted access in 1993, Indian companies have raised about Rupees 31,000 million through American Depository receipts/ Global Depository receipts.

As a result of the reform process, the Indian stock market is in a strong position vis-à-vis securities market of the developed and emerging markets. India has the number one ranking in terms of listed securities on the exchanges followed by the USA. India is also ranked very high in terms of turnover ratio, total value traded in stock exchanges and market capitalization. However, India's share in total world turnover and worldwide market capitalization is less than 1% as compared to the US share of around 50%. A major attraction for international investors is the relative price stability of Indian securities as compared to other foreign securities.

2.2 MAJOR STOCK MARKETS OF THE WORLD

The stock exchanges of the world differ in terms of size, structure and method of operation. As economies get integrated into a global economy regional stock exchanges strongly react to movements in major stock exchanges of the world. In addition to an understanding of the political, social and economic background of each country, knowledge of the development, structure and working of the principal stock exchange of the world is necessary for successful foreign investment. Further as much of the empirical work on finance is done in the context of major stock exchanges of the world like Nasdaq, the New York Stock

Exchange and the London Stock Exchange, an understanding of the working of these exchanges is essential.

The major stock exchanges in the US are Nasdaq, the New York Stock Exchange (NYSE) and the American stock exchange (AMEX).

<u>National Association of Securities Dealers Automated Quotations (Nasdaq)</u>: The world's first and the largest US electronic stock market, it began trading in February 1971. With approximately 3,200 companies, it lists more companies and on an average, trades more shares per day than any other stock exchange in the world. It is home to companies that are leaders across all areas of business including technology, communications, financial services, media and biotechnology.

<u>New York Stock Exchange (NYSE)</u>: The NYSE is the world's leading and the most technologically advanced equities market. It was founded in 1792 to facilitate the exchange of securities and bonds issued by several states and federal government to finance their war time debts. A broad spectrum of market participants including listed companies, individual investors, institutional investors and member firms created the NYSE market. The name NYSE was however adopted in 1863 only. By 1865, the NYSE moved to its present location in Wall Street. The volume of trading crossed the mark of 1 million shares in the year 1886.

Today NYSE has the reputation of a global market place. On an average day 1.46 billion shares valued at $ 46.1 billion trade on the NYSE. It is an integrated market that efficiently blends the best of floor based auction market trading and automatic execution.

The NYSE is governed by the Board of Directors (BOD) which is independent of NYSE management members and listed companies. The board which consists of 6 to 12 individuals, plus a chairman and a Chief executive officer (CEO), has full fiduciary responsibilities and supervises the exchange's regulation, governance, compensation and internal controls.

Apart from the BOD there is a separate board of Executives (BOE) consisting of 20 to 25 individuals representing NYSE constituents as well as NYSE chairman and CEO which advises the BOD. As a result of such open and transparent organizational structure and high level of participation by buyers and sellers, the NYSE is today one of the most competitive venue for trading its listed stocks, providing investors with the lowest cost, deepest liquidity and best prices.

The American Stock Exchange (AMEX): It stands second to the NYSE in terms of the volume of transactions. The AMEX is an auction market where trading is conducted through a centralized specialist system. By combining a specialist based auction market with state of the art trading technology- the foundation of a fair, efficient and accountable marketplace- all trades are executed swiftly with reliability, accuracy and transparency. By centralizing order flow and giving public orders priority over professional trading investors trade on a level playing field and the achieve the best price available. Trading is more orderly so price volatility is reduced, spreads are narrower and execution costs are lower.

The London Stock Exchange: One of the oldest stock exchanges in the world, in terms of number and range of national and international securities traded and in size of membership it occupies pre-eminent position. It has a very high ranking in terms of total value of transactions and has a broad and significantly free stock market. The large volume of business, longer trading period, easily available accurate information, a growing share owning population all these have contributed to a high degree of stability in the share price movements.

Due to the emergence of the joint stock companies, trading in stocks and share started in Britain in the 17th century. Legally the LSE was established in 1802. The LSE is governed by a set of rules and regulations which is published by the secretary to the council of the stock exchange. The council has 36 members of which, except the government broker, all are elected from and by the members of the stock exchange for a period of 3 years. In the administration of the stock exchange the council is assisted by various committees. In addition to the LSE there are four more stock exchanges in UK. All these exchanges are guided by the same rules and regulations.

Tokyo Stock Exchange (TSE): the TSE was established on 15th May 1878 and trading began on June 1st. The influence of World War II was seen in terms of the stock exchange being run as a war-controlled institutions and suspension of trading for a brief period.

On 1st April 1949, three stock exchanges were established in Tokyo, Osaka and Nagoya and a few more were added later on. The year 2000 saw some of the stock exchanges merge into TSE. On November 1 2001, TSE Inc. was established after dematerialization of TSE.

The TSE is run by a Board of Directors numbering 10, who take care of the actual management of the TSE. In order to increase the transparency and accountability of management to raise the legitimacy of operations and to fortify the board's supervisory function five of the directors are external board members. The BOD supervises business operations in accordance with corporate policies and is supported by advisory committees composed of market participants and third parties.

2.3 THE INDIAN STOCK MARKET - A BRIEF HISTORY

While the origin of Indian securities market may be traced back to 1875, trading activity in debt securities of East India Company is known to have started by the end of eighteenth century. By 1830, trading began in corporate securities mainly those of cotton presses and banks. The volume and value of business registered remarkable increase. The trading list further widened in 1839 and included securities of banks and business ventures like 'Bengal bonded warehouse docking Company' and the 'Steam Tug Company'. In 1850, the companies act was enacted which introduced the principle of limited liability. This period also witnessed the development of railways, telegraphs and improvement in communication systems. This led to the growth of joint stock companies. The brokerage business became attractive and by 1860 the number of brokers in Bombay increased to 60 from a mere 6 in 1850.

Between 1860 and 1865 there was a boom in the market for securities. The American civil war hindered the supply of cotton from US to Europe and consequently the demand for cotton from India rose. Cotton and cotton related industries went public to raise capital so as to expand their capacities and meet this increased demand. Exporters of cotton goods received bullion and this added to the wealth of Bombay. This wave of prosperity opened avenues for new ventures. The market price of almost all the securities (of both old and new ventures) commanded hefty premium between 1861 and 1865. In fact there was some sort of share mania during this period.

With the end of the American civil war the boom collapsed. The premium vanished and the price of the securities declined steeply. Companies went bankrupt and were dissolved. The investing public was left holding a huge mass of unsaleable papers. The worst came on 1st July 1865, which is popularly known as the 'Black Friday, when hundreds of bonds matured which no one was in a position to redeem.

The depression was long and severe and caused widespread desolations. The brokers, who were a privileged class during the boom time, were taken to be a social nuisance during the depression. They formed an informal association to protect their interests. Finally on 3rd December 1887, they formed a society which was to be India's first stock exchange. This stock exchange was formally established in Dalal Street in Bombay under the name of 'native share and stock brokers' association.

Like Bombay in Ahmedabad too the establishment of cotton textile units led to the creation of Ahmedabad share and stock brokers' association. The exchange was organized as a voluntary non-profit making association and followed the rules and practices prevalent in Bombay stock exchange.

The swadeshi movement in the 20th century gave birth to a new class of Indian entrepreneurs. Rapid development in transport and communication provided further impetus to industrialization. The Calcutta stock exchange association was formed on 15th June 1908, though it is reported that the trading business was carried on even as early as the end of the 18th century. In the initial years the exchange had to face a number of problems.

With the outbreak of World War I, the share prices again registered a rise. During the war the import of goods into India ceased and this gave the impetus to the domestic industry. Almost all enterprises earned profits and declared high dividends. The boom revived the interest of the public in the stock market.

The boom was over by 1921. Faced with foreign competition many domestic industries collapsed and share prices declined. Meanwhile on 6th April 1921, the Madras stock exchange was established. But it soon went out of existence being unable to withstand the severity of depression. Later in 1937 a stock exchange was established.

As already noted during the depression a large number of companies were liquidated leading to a huge waste of public money. In 1923 the government of Bombay appointed a committee under the chairmanship of Atley to look into the working of the BSE and suggest measures to improve its functioning.

The company reported that the chief weakness of BSE was laxity in administration. On its recommendation, the government of Bombay proposed to give monopoly of organized trading in securities to the BSE and in return wanted the rule making powers of the exchange to be vested with the authorities. However the exchange did not want any outside interference and turned down the offer. The government therefore, enacted the Bombay securities control act 1925 to protect the interests of the investing public. Through this act the government empowered itself the right to grant and withdraw recognition to a stock exchange. It also provided that rules and regulations of the stock exchange could only be made or amended subject to the government approval. BSE was granted official recognition on the 14th May 1927.

The 1925 act was however highly ineffective and failed to handle market position during the crisis in 1928, 1933, and 1935. This led to public criticism and demand for inquiry into the working of the BSE. Accordingly, the Morrison committee was set up in 1936, but its recommendations were not implemented due to the outbreak of World War II.

The war again gave a big boost to the stock exchanges. However in 1947 the stock market was in doldrums due to a number of factors like the RBI's directive asking scheduled banks to suspend the extension of credit against stocks and shares, threat of nationalization, spiralling prices and general political uncertainity.

In 1948, the government set up a departmental committee, the draft of which was referred to an expert committee headed by Mr. A. D. Gorwala. On the basis of recommendations of this expert committee, the government enacted the Securities Contract (Regulation) Act 1956. The act permits only those stock exchanges which have been granted recognition by the central government to function and empower the government to control, regulate and supervise the exchanges.

In the post-independent period many new stock exchanges were established. The Delhi stock exchange was established in 1947, followed by Bangalore stock exchanges in 1957 and Cochin 1979. In the eighties stock exchanges were established at Pune, Ludhiana, Guwahati and Patna.

Based on the recommendations of the Pherwani committee, NSE was promoted by leading financial institutions at the behest of the government of India to provide access to investors from all across the country on an equal footing. Unlike other stock exchanges in the country NSE was incorporated as a tax paying company in November 1992.

On its recognition as a stock exchange under the Securities Contracts (Regulations) Act 1956 in April 1993, NSE commenced operations in the wholesale debt market (WDM) segment in June 1994. The capital market (equities) segment commenced operation in November 1994 and operations in the derivative segment commenced in June 2000.

Today NSE is India's leading stock exchange covering various cities and towns across the country. The exchange has brought about unparalleled transparency, speed, efficiency, safety and market integrity. It has set up facilities that serve as a model for the securities industry in terms of systems, practices and procedures

Establishment of SEBI

A major reason for the general public shifting away from investing in stock market is the perception that stock exchanges function as a private club of the brokers. Sensing the need for the presence of watchdog to prohibit fraudulent and unfair trade practices relating to securities market and also check insider trading in securities, the government of India established the 'Securities and Exchange Board of India (SEBI) in April 1988. It was upgraded as a fully autonomous body (a statutory body) in the year 1992 with the passing of the SEBI act on 30th Jan 1992. The basic objectives of the board were identified as protecting the interest of investors and regulate and promote the development of the securities market.

SEBI has introduced comprehensive regulatory measures, prescribed registration norms the eligibility criteria the code of obligations and the code of conduct for different intermediaries like bankers to issue, merchant bankers, brokers and sub-brokers, registrars, portfolio managers, credit rating agencies, underwriters and others. It has framed by-laws, risk identification and risk management systems for clearing houses of stock exchanges, surveillance system etc., which has made dealing in securities both safe and transparent to the end investor.

2.4 REFORMS IN THE INDIAN SECURITIES MARKET

The securities scam of 1992 and 200-02 highlighted the loopholes in the system that has been exploited by manipulating brokers. With the objective of improving the market efficiency, enhancing transparency, preventing unfair trade practices and bringing the Indian market up to international standards many measures of reforms were undertaken. The market today uses state-of-the-art information technology to provide an efficient and transparent trading, clearing and settlement mechanisms and has witnessed several innovations in products and services via demutualization of stock exchange governance, screen based trading, compression of settlement cycles, dematerialization and electronic transfer of securities, security lending and borrowing, professionalization of trading members, fine tuned risk management systems, emergence of clearing corporations to assume counterparty risks, market of debt and derivative instruments and intensive use of information technology.

Some of the reform measures are noted below:

1. <u>DIP guidelines</u>: With the repeal of the Capital Issues (Control) Act 1947, in May 1992, governments control over issue of capital, pricing of the issues, fixing of premia and rates of interest on debentures etc. ceased. Thereafter the market has been allowed to allocate resources among the competing uses. In the interest of investors SEBI issued Disclosures and Investor Protection (DIP) guidelines. These guidelines contain a number of requirements for issuers/intermediaries with a broad intention to ensure that all concerned observe high standards of integrity and fair dealing. The guidelines also aim to secure fuller disclosure of relevant information about the issuer and the nature of the securities to be issued. This enables the investors' to take informed decisions. For example issuers are required to disclose any material 'risk factors' and give justification of pricing in their prospectus. The guidelines cast a responsibility on the lead managers to issue a due diligence certificate stating that they have examined the prospectus and it brings out all the facts and does not contain anything wrong on misleading. Issuers are now required to comply with the guidelines and then asses the market. The companies can access the market only if they fulfill minimum eligibility norms in terms of their track record of distributable profits and net worth.

2. <u>Screen based trading</u>: Prior to 1990s the trading on stock exchanges in India used to take place through an open outcry system. This system did not allow immediate matching or recording of trades. This was time consuming and imposed limits on trading. In order to provide efficiency, liquidity and transparency NSE introduced a nation-wide on-line fully automated screen based trading system (SBTS). In this system a member can punch into the computer quantities of securities and the prices at which he desires to transact and the transaction is executed as soon as it finds a matching sale

or buy order from a counter party. SBTS electronically matches orders on price/time priority and hence it cuts down on time and cost. It enables market participants to see the full market on real time basis, making the market transparent. It allows a large number of participants irrespective of their geographical locations to trade with one another simultaneously improving the debt and liquidity of the market. Following NSE other stock exchanges have also adapted SBTS.

3. <u>Trading cycle</u>: Initially the trading cycle varied from 14 days for specified securities to 30 days for others and settlement took another fortnight. Often this cycle was not adhered to and on several occasions led to defaults and risks in settlements. In order to reduce large open positions, trading cycle was reduced over a period of time to a week. The exchanges however continued to have different weekly trading cycles which enabled shifting of positions from one exchange to another. Rolling settlement on T+5 basis was introduced in respect of specified scrips reducing the trading cycle to one day. It was made mandatory for all exchanges to follow a uniform weekly trading cycle in respect of scrips not under rolling settlement. All scrips moved to rolling settlement from December 2001. The settlement period has been reduced progressively from T+5 to T+3 days. Currently T+2 days is being followed.

4. <u>Derivatives trading</u>: To assist market participants to manage risks better through hedging, speculation and arbitrage the ban on options on securities was lifted in 1995. However trading in derivatives took off much later after the suitable legal and regulatory framework was put in place. Derivatives trading commenced in June 2000 in the Indian securities market on NSE and BSE only. The market presently offers index futures and index options on three indices and stock options and stock futures on individual stocks and futures in interest rate products like notional 91-day T bills and notional 10 year bonds.

5. <u>Demutualization</u>: Historically, brokers owned, controlled and managed the stock exchanges. Therefore regulators focused on reducing the dominance of trading members in the management of stock exchanges. They advised them to reconstitute their governing councils to provide for at least 50% non-broker representation. However, this did not materially alter the

situation. In the face of extreme volatility in the securities market in 2000, the government proposed to corporatize the stock exchanges by which the ownership, management and trading membership would be segregated from one another. A few exchanges have already initialized demutualization process. NSE, for instance, has adopted a pure demutualized governance structure where ownership, management and trading are with three different sets of people and thus completely eliminating any conflict of interest.

6.   <u>Depositories Act</u>: The physical settlement system gave rise to settlement risk. This was due to the time taken for settlement and due to the physical movement of papers. Further the transfer of shares in favor of the purchaser by the company also consumed considerable amount of time. To obviate these problems the Depositories Act, 1996, was passed to provide for the establishment of depositories in securities with speed and accuracy. This act brought in changes by: a) making securities of public limited companies freely transferable subject to certain exceptions; b) dematerializing of securities in the depository mode; and c) providing for maintenance of ownership records in a book entry form. In order to streamline both the stages of settlement process the act envisages transfer of ownership of securities electronically by book entry without making the securities move from person to person. In order to promote dematerialization the regulator has been promoting settlement in demat form in a phased manner in an ever-increasing number of securities.

The stamp duty in the transfer of demat securities has been waived. There are two depositories in India- National Securities Depository Limited (NSDL) and Central Depository Services Limited (CDSL). They have been set up to provide instantaneous electronic transfer of securities. At the end of March 2004 the number of companies connected to NSDL and CDSL were 5,212 and 4,720 respectively. The number of dematerialized securities increased to 97.70 billion at the end of March 2004 from 76.9 billion as of end March 2003.As on the same date, the value of dematerialized securities was Rs 10,701 billion and the number of investor accounts was 5,832,552. All actively traded scrips are held in demat form. Demat settlement accounts for over 9% of turnover settled by delivery. This has almost eliminated the bad deliveries and associated problems.

To prevent certificates from sneaking into circulation it has been made mandatory that all securities should be compulsorily traded in dematerialized form. The admission to a depository for dematerialization of securities has been made a prerequisite for making a public or rights issue or an offer for sale. It has also been made compulsory for public listed companies for making IPO of any security for Rupees 10 crores or more only in dematerialized form.

7. <u>Risk management</u>: with a view to avoid any kind of market failures, the regulator/exchanges have developed a comprehensive risk management system, which is constantly monitored and upgraded. It encompasses capital adequacy of members, adequate margin requirement, limits on exposure and turnover, indemnity, insurance, online position monitoring and automatic disablement etc. They also administer an efficient market surveillance system to detect and prevent price manipulation. The clearing corporation has also put in place a system which tracks online real time client level portfolio based upfront margining. Exchanges have set up trade/settlement guarantee funds for meeting shortages arising out of non-fulfillment/partial fulfillment of funds obligations by the members in a settlement. As a part of the risk management system, index based market wide circuit breakers have also been put in place. The National Clearing Corporation of India Limited (NSCCL) and Bank of Shareholding Limited (BOISL) clearing corporation houses of NSE and BSE, respectively, assume the counter-party risk of each member and guarantees settlement through a fine-tuned risk management system and an innovative method of on-line position monitoring. It also ensures the financial settlement of trades on the appointed day and time irrespective of default by members to deliver the required funds and/or securities with the help of a settlement guarantee fund (SGF). The SGF operates like a self-insurance mechanism wherein members contribute to the fund. In the event of failure of a trading member to meet his obligations, the fund is utilized to thee extent required for successful completion of the settlement. This has eliminated the counter-party risk of trading on the exchange.

8.   <u>Investor protection</u>: To protect the interest of the investor SEBI has made it mandatory to disclose critical data in specified formats. The central government has established a fund called Investor Education and Protection Fund (IEPF) in October 2001 for the promotion of awareness amongst investors and protection of the interest of the investors. DEA, DCA, SEBI and the stock exchanges have set up investor grievance cells for redressal of investor grievance. The exchanges and DCA have all set up investor protection funds to take care of investor claims. All these agencies and investor associations organize investor education and awareness programs.

9.   <u>Globalization</u>: Indian securities market is getting increasingly integrated with the rest of the world. Indian companies have been permitted to raise resources from abroad through issue of American Depository Receipts (ADRs) and Global Depository Receipts (GDRs). Further foreign companies are allowed to invest in Indian companies. FIIs have been permitted to invest in all types of securities including governmental securities. The investments by FIIs enjoy full capital account convertibility. They can invest in a company under portfolio investment route up to 24% of the paid-up capital of the company. This can be increased up to the sectoral cap/statutory ceiling, as applicable. The Indian stock exchanges have been permitted to set up trading terminals abroad. The RBI has also permitted free conversion of ADRs/GDRs into underlying domestic shares and their re-conversion to ADRs/GDRs depending on the direction of price change in the stock. This increases liquidity in ADR/GDR market and aligns ADR/GDR prices with the company's domestic share prices.

2.5 SUGGESTIONS FOR FURTHER REFORMS

Though the above mentioned reform measures have given a competitive edge to the Indian stock markets in the global arena, further fine-tuning is required to keep up the momentum.

1. A large number of regional stock exchanges were set up in the post independence period to take care of regional aspirations. Most of these bourses however compete for the same set of securities through convoluted structures and subsidiaries that go against the concept of transparency and efficiency. The government should close smaller bourses which have no clear future or plans. Merging with a bigger stock exchange is also a viable alternative.

2. The recently launched Indonext should be actively promoted as a bourse with different structure and regulations that fulfills the need for a specialized market for small and medium stocks. Indonext can only work with highly innovative marketing and much greater investment by the bourses in market making, supervision and checking the background and business model of companies listed in this segment.

3. After the Initial Public Offerings (IPO) scam of 1992-1994, when companies vanished with investor's money, SEBI had come out with stringent disclosure norms so that retail investors can make informed decisions. It has also been suggested that SEBI form specific guidelines to regulate or prohibit prospectuses of dubious companies attempting to raise public money. However, it is now felt that IPO clearances cannot be based on disclosures alone and IPO ratings can prove useful in guiding investors. Such ratings should be by independent credit rating agencies, the cost of which can be borne by IEPF (Investor Education and Protection Fund). These ratings commissioned by IEPF will have the advantage of being independent of company influences. Moreover, as credit rating agencies will have to stake their reputation on a proper rating that ensures investor protection, investors will get a fair idea of the work of their investment.

3. The role of banking sector in various scams also makes it imperative for SEBI to have better coordination with the RBI to check the role of banks in aiding and abetting unscrupulous promoters.

4. Window dressing of financial statements of companies is another area that needs to be examined. Independent auditing of accounts of companies will improve the quality of information and allow investors to undertake investment decisions objectively.

5. The market regulator SEBI has also come in for lot of criticisms in its failure to prevent mal-practices in the market. SEBI badly needs to improve administration and accountability and restore its credibility as a powerful regulator. The justice M.H. Kania committee set up to suggest changes to the SEBI Act has made recommendations that clarify the rights and powers of the regulator. An important recommendation of this committee is to empower SEBI to file winding-up petitions against intermediary firms on the lines of powers available under the RBI act and the banking regulation Act.

6. Another noteworthy recommendation of the committee is to grant SEBI some power over the professionals to the extent that those caught indulging in malpractices or certifying false information can be barred from appearing in proceedings before the regulator.

7. It is also imperative that both stock exchanges and SEBI have well designed Management Information Systems. SEBI has to insure that its files and internal data bases are maintained accurately and efficiently. Though SEBI has granted Unique Identification Number (UIN) using biometric techniques for market participants, its data base is not properly maintained to provide names and address of brokers and sub-brokers.

Thus, these reform measures, if implemented, would improve the functioning of Indian stock markets and enable them to attract more funds both from domestic and foreign participants.

CHAPTER 3: ASSET PRICING IN THE MARKET

This chapter discusses the various asset pricing models commonly used in financial literature. **Section 3.1** introduces the concept of market efficiency. **Section 3.2** is devoted to CAPM and discusses the early tests of Sharpe-Linter and Black versions. **Section 3.3** examines the Gibbons, Ross and Shankeen (1989) test for the ex-ante efficiency of any given portfolio in a multivariate framework. Merton's ICAPM and conditional CAPM are discussed in **Section 3.4**. To improve the performance of CAPM, researchers modified the simple risk-return relationship to include skewness and conditional heteroskedasticity in returns. The consequences of the choice of a normal period to estimate a stock's expected returns as also the choice of measure of returns has significant effect on the outcome of any study. These aspects are discussed in **Section 3.5**. The CAPM has been consistently faced with the challenge of explaining various anomalies to the returns behavior. Multifactor asset pricing models were developed to deal with such challenges. In **Section 3.6** we elaborate on the Fama and French three-factor model, a popular model for explaining cross-sectional variations in average returns. **Section 3.7** gives a brief outline of APT. Lastly, the empirical estimation of Fama and French three-factor model is reported in **Section 3.8**.

3.1 EFFICIENT MARKET

In the financial literature the idea of efficiency is considered at three levels. In its weak form markets are said to be efficient when past price changes do not help investors in making profitable investment strategies. The semi-strong form of efficiency refers to a situation when prices factor in all publicly available information, and investors cannot achieve excess returns by trading on any publicly available information. The strong form of efficient market postulates that the current price reflects all relevant information and investors cannot outperform the market even with access to private information.

In an efficient market the real price P_t of a share at the beginning of the time period t is given by

$$P_t = \sum_{k=0}^{\infty} \gamma^{k+1} E_t D_{t+k} \qquad 0<\gamma<1 \quad \ldots\ldots\ldots\ldots\ldots(3.1)$$

where D_t is the real dividend paid at the end of the time t, E_t represents mathematical expectation conditional on information available at time t, and γ is the constant real discount factor. Further $\gamma = \dfrac{1}{(1+r)}$ where r is the constant real interest rate and is also equal to the constant expected rate of return. While equation (3.1) is in ex ante terms, in empirical applications the model is applied in the ex-post form. Thus,

$$P_t = E_t(P^*_t)$$

where P^*_t is the present value of actual subsequent dividends.

This valuation model, therefore, implies that movements in stock prices are related to 'new information' about future dividends. The expected stream of dividends is highly subjective and will vary from investor to investor. The values of 'r' and 'g'- the rate of growth of dividend, are usually viewed as share's fundamental factors, and a change in the market estimate of either will cause the share price to change. Neither 'r' nor 'g' can be scientifically valued, and what is relevant is their market estimated values. If these values change, for whatever reason, then the share price will change accordingly. A rise in 'r' will depress the share price while a rise in 'g' will raise the share price.

The estimated values of 'r' and 'g' vary across individuals and this leads to different valuations of a share price. Some investors may find the current price overvalues the shares while others may find that this undervalues the shares.

Thus, market efficiency must be tested jointly with a model for expected returns. Inferences about market efficiency then become sensitive to the assumed model for expected returns.

In the literature various asset pricing models like Capital Asset Pricing Model (CAPM), conditional CAPM, Inter-temporal CAPM (ICAPM) and Arbitrage Pricing Theory (APT) are employed to estimate the required rate of return for a security. While a validation of these pricing models indicates the market price to be efficient, the reverse is not true. In many situations in rejecting a given asset pricing model, it is difficult to tell whether the risk return relation represented by these models is incorrect or the market is inefficient.

3.2 THE THEORY OF CAPITAL ASSET PRICING MODEL (CAPM)

The CAPM is one of the most extensively studied models both theoretically and empirically for valuation of securities. The CAPM was simultaneously and independently developed by Sharpe (1964), Lintner (1965) and Mossin (1966) following the basic lead of Markowitz (1959) who formulated portfolio selection as a problem of utility maximization under conditions of uncertainity.

The CAPM is a theory about the way stocks are priced in relation to their risk. The underlying logic of the theory is that assets with the same risk should earn the same expected returns. The CAPM put forward the idea that in market equilibrium assets earn premia over the riskless rate that increases with their risk, where the determining influence on risk premia is the covariance between the asset and the so called market portfolio rather than the own or intrinsic risk of an asset.

3.2.1 Asset Market equilibrium

One of the central assumptions of CAPM is that the market is dominated by risk-averse investors who practice optimal diversification to maximize their returns. The basic form of CAPM further postulates that all investors have the same expectations concerning the returns on various securities and the variances and covariances of these returns. Transaction costs and taxes are ignored throughout. In its basic form the model also abstracts from the complexities of 'real time' income and spending decisions. Its derivation is structured on the basis that all investors have the same single period investment horizon over which the real interest rate is fixed. Individuals are assumed to borrow or lend at that rate at no risk regardless of the amount they need to optimize their portfolio decisions.

Under these assumptions a frontier portfolio consisting of risky assets and the riskless asset is identified which minimizes the variance of returns for any given level of expected returns. By choosing a given portfolio `X' consisting of risky assets, and mixing it with varying proportions of investment in the riskless asset an investor can achieve any desired level of portfolio risk. A zero risk investment entails lending out the entire wealth at the risk-free rate. Investors desirous of higher expected returns would put all the wealth in the portfolio `X', thereby increasing their exposure to risk.

If A represents the proportion placed in the portfolio of equities and 1-A the proportion loaned out at the risk-free rate `R_f', the expected return and risk of the joint portfolio would be

$$E(R_P) = (1 - A)R_f + AE(R_X),$$
$$V_P = (1 - A)0 + AV_X \qquad \ldots\ldots\ldots\ldots\ldots\ldots\ldots\ldots\ldots.(3.2)$$

where $E(R_X)$ and V_X are the expected return and variance of the portfolio of risky assets. The risk-return trade-off available by choosing different proportions of risk-free lending and equities portfolio `X', are therefore shown to be the straight line R_fX in Figure 3.1.

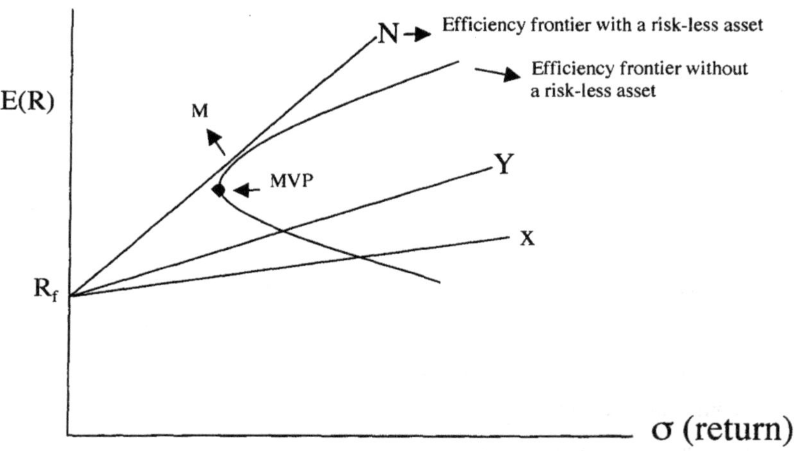

Figure 3.1   The efficiency frontier with borrowing and lending

This trade-off line may be improved, however, by choosing a different portfolio (such as Y) with which to mix the risk-free investment. The line R_fY shows a steeper trade-off as it offers a greater increase in expected return for every unit of additional risk. The steepest trade-off curve possible will be obtained by selecting the portfolio of risky assets that lies exactly where a line from the point R_f is tangent to the efficient frontier. In Figure 3.1 this portfolio corresponds to the risk return combination M.

An even better risk-return trade off is possible by borrowing money at the known interest rate and investing it in the portfolio M. In this case the expected return and the associated variance would be

$$E(R_P) = (1 + A) \, E(R_M) - AR_f$$
$$V_P = (1 + A)V_M + A \, 0 \qquad \cdot \quad \dots\dots\dots\dots\dots(3.3)$$

where AR_f is the interest payment on the borrowing $E(R_M)$ and V_M are the expected return and variance of portfolio M. These opportunities are equivalent to a right-ward continuation of the straight line running through M to N. The MVP shown in Fig 3.1 is the Minimum Variance Portfolio or the portfolio with the lowest possible level of standard deviation.

When it is possible to borrow and lend at a known real rate of interest, the efficient frontier becomes the straight line R_fMN. If investors are operating on the segment R_fM then they are lending/buying risk-free asset while on the segment MN they are borrowing/selling the risk-free asset. Since all investors hold the same risky portfolio M and the riskless asset, though in differing combinations, one can say that the market for risky assets will be out of equilibrium unless M is the market portfolio.

The risk-averse individuals prefer higher expected return given the variance of return and lower variance of return given the expected return. This preference for higher expected return and aversion for variance on the part of the individuals would yield a family of positively sloping convex indifference curves in the standard deviation-expected rate of return space.

While the indifference curve represents the preference of the investors, the efficiency frontier depicts the available mean and standard deviation of the return combination. The optimal portfolio of an individual would be represented by the point of tangency between his indifference curve and the portfolio frontier- an outcome of his net-worth and attitude towards risk. Figure 3.2 shows the case of an investor holding an optimal portfolio consisting of the market portfolio M.

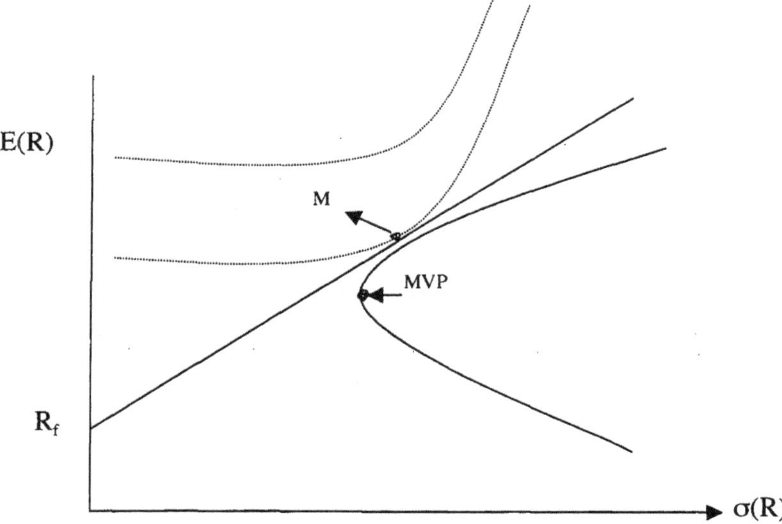

Figure 3.2 Optimal Portfolio of an Investor

As all investors will hold the same portfolio M and the risk-less asset, though in difference combinations, this means that risk preference will have no effect on the best mix of individual equities. This result is known as the 'Separation theorem' because it implies that the decision of how much total risk to accept is separate from the decision of what equities to buy.

The straight line efficient frontier is known as the 'Capital Market Line' (CML) and its equation is written as

$$E(R_P) = R_f + [E(R_M) - R_f]\frac{\sigma_p}{\sigma_M} \ldots\ldots\ldots(3.4)$$

where σ_p and σ_M are the standard deviation of chosen and market portfolio. The CML indicates the amount of extra return offered by the market for every additional point of systematic risk in the portfolio. The unsystematic component of the volatility of an individual stock will net out when mixed with the large number of stocks in the portfolio. The correct measure of how much risk a stock on net brings to the portfolio M will be proportional to the covariance between fluctuations in its return and fluctuations in the return on all other stocks in the portfolio. Specifically this will be measured by the covariance between an individual stock i and the portfolio M expressed per unit of the portfolio variance (σ_M^2). This is also known as 'β' of the stock and is a measure of the stock's systematic risk. A beta of greater than 1 is indicative of a stock being aggressive in the sense that when the market moves in a particular direction it is likely to be moving even faster in the same direction. Similarly, stocks with betas less than one are viewed as defensive stocks in that they move proportionally less in any particular direction than the portfolio as a whole. The market portfolio itself moves exactly in proportion to its own fluctuations and has a beta equal to one.

The return compensation for holding a stock is then equal to R_f plus β times $E(R_M) - R_f$. Thus

$$E(R_i) = R_f + \beta_{iM}[E(R_M) - R_f] \quad\text{..............}(3.5)$$

where $E(R_i)$ is the expected return on stock i.

This is the equation of CAPM as developed by Sharpe and Lintner. Since $E(R_M)$ has to be greater than R_f for investors to bear risk, $E(R_i)$ and β_{iM} are positively related. This is the well known linearity implication of the CAPM and this is depicted by what is called the 'Security Market Line' as shown in Figure 3.3

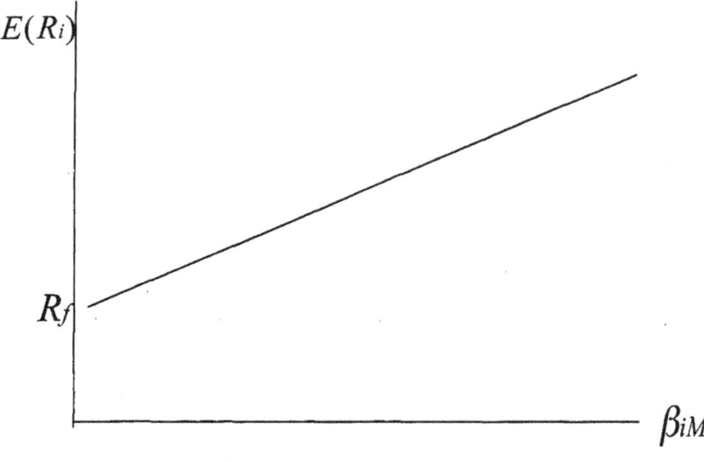

Figure 3.3 Security Market Line

3.2.2 Zero-beta CAPM

A more general formulation of the theory is given without the assumption of a risk-less rate of return and is known as the zero-beta CAPM. With inflation there is no such thing as a risk-free asset. To overcome this difficulty Black (1972) presented a CAPM where there is no risk-free asset yet β remains the correct risk measure. Briefly, the risk-free asset is replaced by a zero β portfolio (Z), whose return shows no systematic correlation with the market. Though in reality most stocks are positively correlated with general movement in the market to some degree it is possible to construct a zero β portfolio by selling some stocks short, thereby losing money when these stocks rise in price and gaining money when their price fall. It is therefore, possible to create return streams that are negatively correlated with the market even when the stock price itself is positively correlated.

The relation between E(R) and market β of Black and Sharpe-Lintner versions differ only in terms of what each says about $E(R_{ZM})$ –the expected return on assets uncorrelated with the market. The Black version requires that $E(R_{ZM})$ must be less than $E(R_M)$, so the premium for β is positive. In contrast in the Sharpe-Lintner version $E(R_{ZM})$ must be R_f and the premium per unit of β risk is

$E(R_M) - R_f$. Both approaches, however, use similar econometric methodologies.

3.2.3 Empirical Model for Testing the CAPM

Tests of the CAPM are based on three implications of the relation between expected return and the market β implied by the model. First, expected returns on all assets are linearly related to their betas and no other variable has marginal explanatory power. Second, the β premium is positive. Third, in the Sharp-Lintner version assets uncorrelated with the market have expected returns equal to the risk-free rate of interest and the β premium is the expected market return minus the risk-free rate.

The econometric testing of CAPM has resulted in a vast literature starting from the late 1960s. Most tests of these predictions use either cross-section or time series regressions. The early cross-section regression tests focused on the Sharpe-Lintner model predictions about the intercept and slope in the relation between expected returns and market beta. A cross-section regression of average asset return on estimated betas is run and the model is tested for the intercept being equal to R_f and the coefficient on beta being equal to $E(R_M) - R_f$.

These tests, however, suffered from two sets of problems. First estimates of β for individual assets are imprecise, creating a measurement error problem when they are used to explain average returns. Second the regression residuals have common sources of variation such as industry effects in average returns. Positive correlation in the residuals produces downward bias in the usual OLS estimates of the standard error of the cross-section of regression slopes.

To improve the precision of estimated betas researchers such as Blume (1970), Friend and Blume (1970) and Black, Jenson and Scholes (1972) worked with portfolios rather than individual securities. Since expected returns and betas combine in the same way in portfolios, if the CAPM explains security returns it also explains portfolio returns. Estimates of betas for diversified portfolios are more precise than estimates for individual securities. Thus, using portfolios in cross-section regression of average returns on betas reduces the critical errors-in-variables problem. Grouping however shrinks the range of betas and reduces statistical power. To mitigate this problem, researchers sort securities on beta when forming portfolios.

Assets are grouped into portfolios on the basis of betas calculated using time series of individual asset returns that do not overlap with the time series of returns used to calculate the group betas. Since asset returns are serially uncorrelated,   measurement errors in these non-contemporaneous betas are also uncorrelated. The estimated betas however have significant correlation. Thus, while variations in betas across groups become substantial, the measurement error within the group becomes uncorrelated across assets.

Fama and Macbeth (1973) proposed a method of addressing the inference problems caused by correlations of the residuals in cross-section regressions. Instead of estimating a single cross-section regression of average monthly return on betas, they estimated month-by-month cross-section regression of monthly returns on betas. The time series means of monthly slopes and intercepts along with the standard error of means are then used to test whether the average premium for beta is positive and whether the average return on assets uncorrelated with the market is equal to the average risk-free interest rate. In this approach the standard error of the average intercept and slope are determined by month-to-month variation in the regression coefficients which fully captures the effects of residual correlation on variation in the regression coefficients, but sidesteps the problem by actually estimating the correlations. The effects of residual correlation are in effect captured via repeated sampling of the regression coefficients.

Jensen (1968) was the first to note that the Sharpe and Lintner (S-L) version of the relation between expected returns and market beta also implies a time series regression tests. The (S-L) CAPM says that the average value of an asset's excess return is completely explained by its average realized CAPM risk premium (β times the average value of $(R_{Mt} - R_{ft})$). This implies that 'Jensen alpha' the intercept term in the time series regression

$$R_{it} - R_{ft} = \alpha_i + \beta_{iM}(R_{Mt} - R_{ft}) + \varepsilon_{it}, \ t = 1....T............(3.6)$$

is zero for each asset.

More commonly, researchers have examined the linearity of the risk-return relation by adapting a two-part regression model. First the regression equation (3.6) is fitted to the time series data, in order to estimate β. In the next stage for each t, a cross-section regression equation

$$Rit - Rft = \gamma_t + \delta_t \beta_i + \mu_{it}, \quad i = 1....N \quad ....(3.7)$$

is fitted where N is the number of portfolio in the sample. The null hypothesis to be tested is $\gamma_t = 0$ and $\delta_t > 0$. This corresponds to the formulation of the 'Security Market Line'.

3.2.4 Results of Empirical Studies

The early tests firmly rejected the S-L version of CAPM. These tests established a positive relation between β and average return, but it was too flat. S-L model predicts that the intercept is R_f and the coefficient on β is $E(R_M) - R_f$. The regressions consistently found that the intercept was greater than the average R_f and the coefficient on β was less than the average excess market returns. This is true in the early tests such as Douglas (1968), Black, Jensen and Scholes (1972), Miller and Scholes (1972), Blume and Friend (1973) and Fama and Macbeth (1973) as well as in the more recent cross-section regression tests like Fama and French (1992).

The evidence that the relation between β and average return is too flat is confirmed in time series tests such as Friend and Blume (1970), Black, Jensen and Scholes (1972) and Stambaugh (1982). The intercepts in the time series regression of excess asset returns on the excess market return are positive for assets with low betas and negative for assets with high betas.

The S-L and Black version of CAPM share the prediction that the market portfolio is mean-variance efficient. This implies that differences in expected returns across securities and portfolios are entirely explained by differences in market beta and other variables should add nothing to the explanation of E(R). Such tests can be carried out by simply adding pre-determined explanatory variables to the month-to-month cross-section regression of return on β as shown by Fama and Macbeth (1973). If all differences in E(R) are explained by β the average slopes on the additional variables should not be reliably different from zero. In this study, the additional variables were squared market beta (to test the prediction that the relation between E(R) and β is linear) and residual variances from regressions of returns on market return (to test the prediction that market beta is the only measure of risk needed to explain E(R). The variables did not add to the explanation of average returns provided by beta. Thus, the authors concluded that their market proxy- an equal weighted portfolio of NYSE stocks- is on the minimum variance frontier.

The hypothesis that market betas completely explain E(R) can also be tested using time series regression. In the time series regression of excess returns of an asset i on the excess market return, the intercept is the difference between the asset's average excess return and the excess return predicted by Sharpe-Lintner model (that is β times the average excess market return). If the model holds there is no way to group assets into portfolios whose intercepts are relatively different from zero. For example, intercepts for a portfolio of stocks with high ratios of earnings/price and a portfolio of stocks with low earning/price ratios should both be zero. In order to test the hypothesis that market betas suffice to explain E(R) one estimates the time series regression for a set of assets (or portfolios) and then jointly tests the vector of regression intercepts against zero. The time series tests of Gibbons (1982) and Stambaugh (1982) showed that the market proxies were on the minimum variance frontier.

These studies thus confirmed the central prediction of the Black version of CAPM i.e. that market betas suffice to explain E(R) and that the risk premium for β is positive. But the more specific prediction of the Sharpe-Lintner CAPM that the premium per unit of β is the expected market return minus the riskless rate was constantly rejected.

A major criticism levied against these studies was the non-observability of the market portfolio (see Roll 1977). In these studies what was literally tested was whether a specific proxy for the market portfolio was efficient in the set of portfolios that can be constructed from it and the left hand side assets used in the test. Whether a market proxy is mean-variance efficient or not is clearly independent of the true 'market portfolio' being mean-variance efficient. It is the latter which is of any consequence to the valuation theory. One might conclude from this that the CAPM has never been tested and prospects for testing are not good because the set of left hand side assets does not include all marketable assets and data for the true market portfolio of all assets are likely beyond reach.

Stanbaugh (1982), however, reported that tests of CAPM are not sensitive to expanding the market proxy beyond common stocks, basically because the volatility of expanded market returns is dominated by the volatility of stock returns. His results, however, have limited acceptance since his market proxies were confined to US assets.

Fama and French pointed out that the problem is not one of finding the market portfolios. They argued that if one can find a market proxy that is on the minimum variance frontier, it can be used to describe differences in expected returns. In their 1998 study, they found that betas for a global stock market portfolio cannot explain the high average returns observed around the world on stocks with high book-to-market or high earnings-price ratios.

3.3 A TEST OF EFFICIENCY OF A GIVEN PORTFOLIO

Subsequent toRolls's critique several researchers explored alternative frameworks to examine the validation of CAPM or its modifications. Shankeen (1987) argued that the fraction of the total market value of all assets included in the proxy for the market is not all that important. Rather, it is the correlation between the proxy return and the market portfolio that counts. If the market proxy is perfectly correlated with the true market portfolio, then it amounts to testing the theory. Kandel and Stambaugh (1987) and Shanken (1987) conducted tests of CAPM conditional on the assumption about correlation between the proxy and the true market portfolio.

3.3.1 Multivariate test of the efficiency of a given portfolio

Gibbons, Ross and Shankeen (1989) provided a highly generalized approach to test for the ex-ante efficiency of any given portfolio. In the particular case when this portfolio happens to be the true market portfolio or a proxy portfolio with a high correlation than it amounts to a test of the Sharpe-Lintner hypothesis.

The regression used in the study is of the following form

$$r_{it} = \alpha_{ip} + \beta_{ip} r_{pt} + \varepsilon_{it} \quad i = 1....N \quad ....(3.8)$$

where

$$r_{it} = R_{it} - R_{ft} \quad \text{(excess return on portfolio i in period t)}$$

$r_{pt} = R_{pt} - R_{ft}$ (excess return on the portfolio whose efficiency is being tested) ε_{it} = disturbance term for the portfolio i in period t.

Here the disturbances are assumed to be jointly normally distributed each period with mean zero and non-singular covariance matrix Σ conditional on the excess return for portfolio p. Disturbances are also assumed to be independent over time. Further r_{pt} and ε_{it}'s are also assumed to be linearly independent.

The test of efficiency of the portfolio is based upon the estimated values of intercept and if these show cross-sectional dependence then the use of univariate test will lead to erroneous inferences. Gibbons et al. (1989) found cross-sectional dependence among the residuals of ten beta-sorted portfolios which they used to study the efficiency of the CRSP equal weighted index during the period 1931 to 1965. They found the residuals of portfolios with similar betas to be positively correlated and those of portfolios with very different betas to be negatively correlated. Similar pattern of correlation was also found in the estimated intercepts. Thus, it becomes difficult to infer about the observed pattern in estimated values of the true parameters. If both α's and ε's show correlation across equations then the dependent variables in the equation (3.8) will also show cross-sectional dependence. Thus, since the intercepts show cross-sectional dependence, a joint significance test of estimated values of intercept across all equations becomes necessary. The need therefore for the use of multivariate regressions.

For mean-variance efficiency, the null hypothesis

$$H_0 : \alpha_{ip} = 0, \, i = 1...N \dots\dots\dots(3.9)$$

should hold. Using a multivariate generalization of the univariate 't test', Gibbon's et al. define Holtelling's T^2 statistic as

$$T^2 = ckd'S^{-1}d \dots\dots\dots(3.10)$$

Here the estimated intercepts of equation (3.8) have a multivariate normal distribution conditional on r_{pt} (t= 1..T), i.e.

$$\sqrt{T/(1+\hat{\theta}_P^2)}\,\hat{\alpha}_P \sim N\left(\sqrt{T/(1+\hat{\theta}_P^2)}.\hat{\alpha}_P, \Sigma \right) \dots\dots\dots(3.11)$$

where T = number of time series observations on returns

$$\hat{\alpha}_p = \left(\alpha_{1p}, \alpha_{2p}, \ldots, \alpha_{Np}\right), \; \hat{\theta}_p = \left(\frac{\bar{r}_p}{S_p^2}\right)$$

$\bar{r}_p$ = sample of r_{pt}

S_p^2 = sample variance of r_{pt} without any adjustment for degrees of freedom.

Further $\hat{\alpha}_p$ and $\hat{\Sigma}$ are independent and (T-2) $\hat{\Sigma}$ has a wishart distribution with parameter (T-2) and Σ. Here $\hat{\Sigma}$ is the unbiased residual covariance matrix.

In the T^2 defined in equation (3.10) s is the sample estimate of the covariance matrix Σ and has a wishart distribution with parameters k & Σ i.e. s~W_f (k,Σ) and d has a f-variate normal distribution with parameters δ and $c^{-1}\Sigma$ i.e. d~N_f (δ, $c^{-1}\Sigma$)

Rewriting T^2 statistic as

$$T^2 = \frac{k d' s^{-1} d}{d' \Sigma^{-1} d} * c d' \Sigma^{-1} d \ldots \ldots \ldots (3.12)$$

for given d

$$\frac{d' \Sigma^{-1} d}{d' s^{-1} d} \sim x^2 (k - f + 1) \ldots \ldots \ldots (3.13)$$

and since

$$d \sim N_f(\delta, c^{-1}\Sigma), \; c d' \Sigma^{-1} d \sim x^2 (f, c \delta' \Sigma^{-1} \delta) \ldots \ldots \ldots (3.14)$$

Thus $\dfrac{T^2}{k}$ is the ratio of non-central χ^2 (f, c $\delta' \Sigma^{-1} \delta$) to a central χ^2 (k- f + 1).

Hence

$$\frac{k-f+1}{f} * \frac{T^2}{k} \sim F\,(f,\ k\text{-}f\text{+}1,\ c\ \delta'\ \Sigma^{-1}\delta)\ldots\ldots\ldots(3.15)$$

This equivalent F test is used in Gibbons et al. model.

The T^2 statistic is now given as

$$T^2 = I\,(T\text{-}2)\left(\sqrt{T/(1+\hat{\theta}_p^2)}\,\hat{\alpha}_p'\right).\left((T-2)\hat{\Sigma}\right)^{-1}.\left(\sqrt{T/(1+\hat{\theta}_p^2)}\,\hat{\alpha}_p\right)$$

Substituting (T-2) for k and N for f in (3.15), the test statistic is given as

$$\frac{T-2-N+1}{N} * T - 2 * \frac{T}{1+\hat{\theta}_p^2} * \frac{\hat{\alpha}_p'\hat{\Sigma}^{-1}\hat{\alpha}_p}{T-2} * \frac{1}{T-2}$$

$$= \frac{(T-N-1)T}{N(T-2)} * \frac{\hat{\alpha}_p'\hat{\Sigma}^{-1}\hat{\alpha}_p}{1+\hat{\theta}_p^2}$$

$$\ldots\ldots\ldots(3.16)$$

This has non-central F distribution with degrees of freedom N and T-N-1. The non-centrality parameter λ is given by

$$\lambda = T\,W_u \ldots\ldots\ldots\ldots\ldots\ldots(3.17)$$

where $$W_u = \frac{\hat{\alpha}_p'\hat{\Sigma}^{-1}\hat{\alpha}_p}{1+\hat{\theta}_p^2}$$

Under the null hypothesis W_u has a central F distribution unconditionally. However, under the alternate the distribution of W_u is conditional on the sample value of r_{pt}. Gibbons et al., therefore, developed another statistic W which has a F distribution with degrees of freedom N and T-N-1 under the null and alternate hypotheses and can therefore be used for drawing statistical inferences. The statistic W is defined as

$$W = \frac{\hat{\alpha}'_p \hat{\Sigma}^{-1}_{MLE} \hat{\alpha}_p}{1 + \hat{\theta}^2_p} \quad \ldots\ldots\ldots(3.18)$$

Gibbons et al. gave another interpretation to the statistic W such that it can be used for understanding the economic significance of the departure from the null hypothesis. In the exercise involving the minimization of variances of the portfolio subject to the constraint of a given level of mean they show that

$$W = \frac{\sqrt{1 + \hat{\theta}^{*2}}}{\sqrt{1 + \hat{\theta}^2_p}} - 1 = \Psi^2 - 1 \quad \ldots\ldots\ldots(3.19)$$

Where $\hat{\theta}^*$ is the maximum excess sample mean return per unit of standard deviation

$\hat{\theta}_P$ is the ratio of ex post average excess return in portfolio p to its standard deviation and Ψ^2 has an F distribution with degrees of freedom N and T-N-1.

Under the null hypothesis Ψ^2 will be close to one because in the estimation of $\hat{\theta}^*$ returns on all assets including portfolio p is considered. When Ψ^2 is sufficiently greater than one then this implies that there exists at least one portfolio whose excess return per unit of standard deviation is greater than that of portfolio P. This would lead to the rejection of the null hypothesis.

Using the above model Gibbons et al. conducted a test for the ex-ante efficiency of CRSP equal weighted index during the period 1931 to 1965 using a data set similar to that used by Black, Jensen and Scholes (1972). The multivariate test does not reject the ex-ante efficiency of the index. This is similar to the conclusion reached by Black et al. It is however possible that univariate and multivariate tests lead to contradictory conclusions and depending on univariate tests when residuals exhibit cross-sectional dependence may lead to erroneous inferences.

The Gibbons et al. test provides an F test on the intercepts that has exact small sample properties. The test, however, is sensitive to the number of portfolios that determine the ex-post efficiency frontier. The power of the test is an increasing function of the non-centrality parameter λ. Gibbons et al. show that

λ is proportional to N and T (with N<T). Thus, for a given T, the power of the test is influenced by the choice of the number of portfolios.

Further the test is also sensitive to the choice of asset sets. The type of subset of assets used affects the conclusions regarding the efficiency of a given index. Thus, for instance for the CRSP value weighted index, while ex-ante efficiency of it during the period 1926 to 1982 is rejected using twelve industry sorted portfolios it is accepted using ten size sorted portfolios at 1% level of significance.

3.4 ICAPM AND CONDITIONAL CAPM

Empirical contradictions of the CAPM forced researchers in the direction of a more complicated asset pricing model. The CAPM is based on many unrealistic assumptions. For example, the assumption that investors care only about the mean and variance of distribution of one period portfolio returns is extreme. It is reasonable that investors also care about how their portfolio returns covaries with labor income and future investment opportunities, so a portfolio's return variance misses important dimensions of risk. If so, market beta is not a complete description of an asset's risk.

Arguing that individuals are not merely investors and they maximize not primarily the returns on their assets, but consumption over their lifetime, Breeden (1979) developed the Consumption CAPM (CCAPM). This version of CAPM considers not just the covariance between particular securities and market portfolio but the covariance between securities and earnings from work.

Another assumption that needs to be reconsidered is the requirement that investors base their decisions on a single period over which the rate of interest on the risk-free asset (or the return on the zero beta portfolio) does not vary. In reality investors tend to have multi-period horizons over which interest rates and expected returns may fluctuate significantly.

Merton (1973) tackled this problem by deriving a version of CAPM that assumed investment and trading occurs continuously over time and that interest rates fluctuate. This formulation results in an equation for the required rate of return on a stock very similar to the security market line, but the addition of a second term involving another beta (β_2). A stock now has systematic risk not only to the extent that its return fluctuates in sympathy with the market portfolio (as measured by β_1) but also to the extent that it is correlated with movements in the risk-free rate. It is this second source of systematic risk that the term involving β_2 allows for.

In Merton's intertemporal capital asset pricing model (ICAPM), investors are concerned not only with their end of period payoff, but also with the opportunities they will have to consume or invest the profit. Thus, when choosing a portfolio at time t-1 ICAPM investors consider how their wealth at t might vary with the future variables like labor income, the prices of consumption goods, and the nature of portfolios opportunities at t and expectations about the labor income, consumption and investment opportunities to be available after t.

Like CAPM investors, ICAPM investors prefer high expected returns and low returns variance. But ICAPM investors are also concerned with the covariances of portfolio returns with other variables. As a result optimal portfolios are 'multifactor efficient' which means that they have the largest possible expected returns, given their return variances and covariances of their return with the other relevant variables.

Researchers have also tried to build dynamism in the model by allowing for time varying betas and expected returns. Chan (1988) found that betas vary with market value and therefore, questioned the testing the procedure of CAPM where betas are estimated over a prior period. The instability of CAPM due to changes in betas was shown by Ball and Kothari (1989) also. They found that equity betas vary with past return because of variations in the market valued leverage. The study concluded that because realized returns affect subsequent expected returns an unbiased control for variation in expected returns is crucial in tests of market efficiency.

That beta values for new issues change over time as investors gather more information on the issuer has been argued by many including Klein and Bawa (1976, 1977), Barry and Brown (1984, 1985), and Clarkson and Thompson (1990).

Jaganathan and Wang (1996) also worked with CAPM that holds in a conditional sense i.e. betas and market risk premium vary over time. They found that this specification, which also includes human capital as part of aggregate wealth, performs well in explaining the cross-section of average returns.

Barberis's (2000) showed the implication of time variation in expected returns for investors making portfolio decisions. Earlier Samulson (1969) and Merton (1969) had shown that if asset returns are i.i.d., an investor rebalancing his portfolio optimally should choose the same asset allocation regardless of investment horizon. However, Barberis reported that with time varying and predictable returns the optimal portfolio allocation for short and long horizons will be very different depending upon whether parameters are assumed to be known with certainity or not.

3.5 PROBLEMS IN THE TESTING OF CAPM

The predictive power of a model is dependent on the set of assumptions made. While Friedman (1953) asserted that assumptions of economic theory are irrelevant there were others who acknowledged the dependence of empirical inference on statistical assumptions. One of the crucial assumptions of CAPM pertains to the normality in the distributions of asset returns. Such normality in returns distribution is necessary to express investors' choice in terms of first and second moments of distribution i.e. mean and variance of returns. While the central limit theorem can be invoked to justify the assumption of normality in portfolio returns as the number of assets in the portfolio increases, the rate and the accuracy with which portfolio returns approaches normality, will influence the validity of CAPM.

Many empirical studies have found stock returns to deviate from normal distribution. Studies by Mandelbrot (1963) and Fama (1965) reported the presence of extreme observations in stock returns resulting in fat-tailed distributions. Such outliers have been found in companies experiencing dramatic firm specific news and smaller companies in general. Lakonishok and Vermaelen (1990) substantiated the belief that underpricing of stocks lead to firms offering stock repurchases when they found substantial negative abnormal returns prior to the announcement of the offer. Earlier Jensen (1986) had also pointed to the effect of dramatic news events on returns when he found companies involved in take-over situations exhibiting extreme performance prior to announcements related to corporate control changes. Roll (1988) in fact showed that R^2 increases significantly when news dates are excluded for firms involved in take-over situations.

Noting the presence of skewness in returns distributions, Harvey and Siddiqui (2000) argued that unconditional return distributions can be adequately characterized only by including the third moment. *Ceteris Paribus* investors should prefer portfolios that are right skewed to portfolios that are left skewed. Hence they pointed out that assets that decrease a portfolio's skewness (i.e. making the portfolio more left skewed) should command higher expected returns as compared to assets that increase a portfolio's skewness and therefore should have lower expected returns. Such asymmetries in portfolio returns arise because of the presence of the limited liability as against a possible unlimited return in equity investments.

Apart from skewness the problem in modeling returns with constant variance has also been highlighted in literature. Time series of financial variables show changing variances. Following Engle (1982) ARCH (Autoregressive Conditional Heterokedasticity) model has been used to capture the influence of past information on forecast variance. A Generalized ARCH (GARCH) disturbance process was later developed by Bollerslov (1986). The GARCH (p, q) process is given by

$$Y_t = \beta X_t + \varepsilon_t \qquad t = 1.....T \ \ldots\ldots\ldots\ldots(3.20)$$
$$\varepsilon_t \mid I_{t-1} \sim N(O, h_t)$$

where $h_t = \alpha_0 + \sum_{i=1}^{p} \alpha_i \varepsilon_{t-1}^2 + \sum_{j=1}^{q} \beta_j h_{t-j}$

and $Y_t \mid I_{t-1} \sim N(\beta X_t, h_t)$

To keep h_t non-negative Bollerslov imposed the condition

$\alpha_0 > 0$, $\alpha_i > 0$, $\beta_i > 0$ $\quad \forall$ i,j

In the ARCH/GARCH process the joint distribution of ε's and y's are not multivariate normal but the conditional distribution of ε's are normal. The marginal distribution of ε's and y's have fatter tails than the normal and in general do not have all moments finite. Thus, during periods of fluctuating economic activity forecasting accuracy of economic agents becomes dependent on the past value of errors. As speculations become riskier, risk-averse agents have to be compensated with higher risk premia for holding risky assets. Thus, conditional means as also conditional expected returns will vary with conditional variance. This is the idea behind ARCH-M model developed by Engle et al. (1987).

Noting that skewness in financial markets varies through time and possesses schematic relation to expected returns and variance, Harvey and Siddiqui (1999) modified the GARCH model to get GARCH (p,q,r) model. Thus the specifications of GARCH (1,1,1) model is given by the following equations

$$h_t = \beta_0 + \beta_1 h_{t-1} + \beta_2 \varepsilon_{t-1}^2$$
$$s_t = \gamma_0 + \gamma_1 s_{t-1} + \gamma_2 \varepsilon_{t-1}^3 \qquad \dots\dots\dots\dots\dots(3.21)$$

Where $h_t = \text{var}_{t-1}[R_{M,t} - R_{f,t}]$ and $s_t = Skew_{t-1}[R_{M,t} - R_{f,t}]$.

To ensure that conditional variances and skewness are non-explosive the following constraints were imposed:

$0<\beta_1<1$, $0<\beta_2,1$, $-1<\gamma_1<1$, $-1<\gamma_2<1$, $\beta_1 + \beta_2< 1$ and $-1<\gamma_1+\gamma_2<1$.

Though the OLS estimation of ARCH class of models gives Best Linear Unbiased (BLU) estimators, asymptomatic efficiency is imposed by using non-linear maximum likelihood method.

Another problem faced by researchers is the choice of return horizon. Many studies focused on returns in short period (a few days) around a clearly dated event. Because the daily expected returns are close to zero, the model for expected return will not have a big effect on inferences about abnormal returns. Measuring returns over such short periods would be justified only if the average holding period were so small i.e. the market were to be dominated by speculators and the full response of prices to an event be short lived. As both the conditions are rarely met in the real world, there is a definite possibility of drawing erroneous inferences. Test of market efficiency for periods of less than one year have found realized returns to have statistically significant but numerically small autocorrelation.

Long-term studies have an edge over short term return studies as they are less susceptible to the effects of thin and non-synchronous trading, bid ask spreads and other micro-structural issues. Levhari and Levy (1977) noted that empirical estimates of the CAPM parameters depended on the investment horizon and claimed that some of the anomalies in the early studies were consistent with their measured return horizon being too short. For instance, Handa et al. (1989) found the evidence on the firm size effect to be sensitive to return horizon. Similarly Kothari et al. (1993) found the book-to-market effect documented by Fama and French (1992) to be sensitive to return horizon. However, the literature reports very little evidence on the performance of multiple beta pricing models over long horizons.

The long-term return studies however, are highly sensitive to choice of models and the way tests are done. While for some events, adjustment of stock prices may be spread over a long post event period there are others for which long periods of unusual pre-event returns are common. Moreover, as will be shown in the behavioral approach to the study of market, stocks can show return continuation in the short run and mean reversion in the long run, the choice of invest horizon can therefore lead to different conclusions. Thus, the choice of a normal period to estimate a stock's expected return becomes problematic.

Since the model of market equilibrium is jointly tested with market efficiency, both will have the same unit of time for returns. If monthly returns are used in the model, price behavior over long periods is usually observed by calculating average monthly abnormal returns (AARs) or sum of average monthly abnormal returns (CARs). However, these measures do not accurately measure the return to an investor who holds a security for a long post event period. Barber & Lyon (1997) showed that the use of AARs or CARs can produce different inferences than buy and hold abnormal returns (BHARs). But as Lyon et al. (1997) noted it is difficult to argue that BHARs inferences are more reliable than AARs or CARs. The reason being average monthly returns avoid the problems of extreme skewness produced by compounding monthly returns to get long term BHARs. Brav (1997) also emphasized that the various methods used for drawing inferences from BHARs fail to correct fully for the correlation of returns across events that is not absorbed by the model used to adjust for expected returns.

Inferences regarding market efficiency in studies involving long-term post event returns get influenced by the weighting rule used in portfolio formation. Studies show that apparent anomalies in long-term post event returns typically shrink a lot and often disappear when event firms are value weighted rather than equal weighted. All the common asset pricing models have systematic problems in explaining the average returns on categories of small stocks. Since equal weight portfolio returns give more weight to small stocks, bad-model problem are more severe in inferences from equal weight returns.

Different methods are used in the literature to measure abnormal return on stocks. In general, abnormal returns are estimated as the difference between an event firm's return and the return on a non-event firm or portfolio that is similar on characteristics known to be related to average returns. Individual event studies show that matching on size produces much different abnormal returns than matching on size and book-to-market value. And size and book-to market value does not capture all relevant cross-firm variation in average returns due to expected returns or sample specific patterns in average returns.

The importance of correct model selection can be brought out clearly if one recognizes that a bad model that produces spurious abnormal average return of x% per month eventually becomes statistically reliable in cumulative monthly abnormal returns. Spurious anomalies will also result if the study period exhibits sample specific patterns in average returns that are due to chance. In such cases even if a 'true' model were to be fitted there would be systematic deviations from the models predictions.

Questions have also been raised on the testing procedures. Elton (1999) argued that using realized returns as a proxy for expected returns may lead to rejection of asset pricing model with a high probability if there are unanticipated information surprises pertaining to the firm or to the priced factor or an un-priced factor. Defining

$$R_t = E_{t-1}(R_t) + \varepsilon_t \quad \ldots\ldots\ldots\ldots(3.22)$$

where $E_{t-1}(R_t)$ is expected return at t conditional on information available at t-1 and ε_t is the unexpected return coming from systematic factors or unique firm specific events. Thus, the justification of using realized returns as a proxy for expected returns rests on the assumption of ε_t's being distributed independently with a mean zero. However, under the circumstances of information surprise being significant R_t would be equal to $E(R_{t-1}) + I_t + \varepsilon_t$ where I_t is a significant information set and represents a jump in the ε_t distribution. In cases of information surprises appropriate grouping techniques can reduce if not eliminate firm specific surprises.

3.6 FAMA AND FRENCH THREE FACTOR MODEL

Starting in the late nineteen seventies empirical work appeared that challenged even the Black version of the CAPM. Fama and French (1992) made a devastating blow to CAPM when they reported that there seemed to be no connection between beta and returns. Earlier Banz (1981) showed that CAPM does not describe expected returns on small stocks. Stattman (1980) and Rosenberg, Reid and Lanstein (1985) documented that stocks with high book-to-market equity ratios have high average returns that are not captured by their betas.

The traditional CAPM also fails to explain the January effect. Carroll et al. (1992) developed a non-linear model to account for the January effect. Examining whether non-linearity in risk return relationship is dependent on the return distribution, the authors compared the traditional CAPM with that of Shalit and Yitzhaki's (1984) mean extended Gini CAPM. The latter is an equilibrium asset pricing relation that is independent of the form of underlying asset distribution.

Their results suggested that non-normality of returns might not be responsible for the non-linearities in risk-return relationship. They reported systematic risk return relationship to be negative in January and positive significant and non-linear in the rest of the year. A significant positive relationship between non-systematic risk and return was reported for January but not for the rest of the year. Thus, this study and similar other studies by Ritter and Chopra (1989), Tinic and West (1986) came to the conclusion that there exists a positive non-linear relationship between risk and return except during January when the market rewards bearing systematic risk.

Such anomalies to the model forced researchers in the direction of multiple factor models (see Basu 1977; Banz 1981; Chan et al. 1991; Fama and French 1992) for explaining cross-sectional variation in expected returns.

In the three-factor model developed by Fama and French, size and ratio of book value of common equity to market equity (BE/ME) are used as proxy for sensitivity to common risk factors in returns. Fama and French argued that the higher average return on small stocks and high book-to-market value stocks reflect unidentified state variables that produce undiversifiable risks (covariances) in returns that are not captured by market returns and are priced separately from market betas. In support of this claim they showed that the return on the stocks of small firms covary more with one another than with returns on the stocks of large firm and returns on high book-to-market (value) stocks covary more with one another than with return on low book-to-market (growth) stocks.

In their 1995 paper Fama and French showed that there are similar size and book-to-market patterns in the covariation of fundamentals like earnings and sales. They formed six portfolios on the basis of values of size and BE/ME for individual stocks. They then examined the behavior of earnings for eleven years i.e. 5 years before and 5 years after firms were ranked on size and BE/ME. They found that high BE/ME stocks were less profitable than low BE/ME stocks for 4 years before and at least 5 years after ranking dates. Similarly, controlling for BE/ME they found small stocks to have lower earnings on book equity than big stocks.

Their analyses also contradicted the analyses of Lakonishok, Shleifer and Vishny (1994). Low BE/ME stocks have high growth and high BE/ME stocks have poor growth in earnings through the year of portfolio formations. LSV then deduced that the market incorrectly extrapolates these earnings growth ignoring their temporary nature. Low BE/ME stocks then have low average returns after portfolio formation because their earnings growth is weaker than the market expects and high BE/ME stocks have high average returns because their earnings growth is stronger than expected. Fama and French however, showed that the ratio of next year earnings to current year price instead of being low in the year after portfolio formation for low BE/ME stocks remain quite stable in the eleven years around portfolio formation and in fact the ratios show a marginal increase beginning in year t=1 [Note: t=0 is the portfolio formation year]

Similarly, the data on high BE/ME stocks also did not correspond to LSV analysis. The study concluded that there are size and book to market factors in earnings like those in returns. However, the authors failed to show that common variation in returns was driven by common factors in earnings.

Fama and French (1996) used their three-factor model to explain many of the CAPM average return anomalies. The model describes expected return on a portfolio in excess of the risk-free rate as a function of: (i) in excess return on a broad market portfolio (R_M-R_f); (ii) the difference between the return on a portfolio of small stocks and the return on a portfolio of large stocks (SMB); and (iii) the difference between the return on a portfolio of high B/M stocks and the return on a portfolio of low BE/ME stocks (HML). In other words, the expected return on portfolio i is

$$E(R_i) - R_f = b_i[E(R_M) - R_f] + S_i E(SMB) + h_i E(HML) \cdots\cdots(3.23)$$

where $E(R_M) - R_f$, E(SMB), E(HML) are expected premiums and the factor sensitivities b_i, S_i and h_i are the slopes in the time series regression

$$R_i - R_f = a_i + b_i(R_M - R_f) + S_i SMB + h_i HML + \varepsilon_i \cdots\cdots(3.24).$$

The study showed that the three-factor model gives a good description of returns in portfolios formed on earnings/price, cash flow/price and sales growth in addition to explaining returns on portfolios formed on size, BE/ME and industry returns.

Though Fama and French model is very popular, critics have questioned the rationale behind using SMB and HML portfolios. Both size and BE/ME are themselves not state variables and are also not related to state variables of any concern to investors. In fact in the same paper Fama and French conceded that any three Multifactor Minimum Variance (MMV) portfolios will do the job of explaining differences in average return. Thus, MMV portfolios formed on BE/ME, EPS/P (ratio of earnings per share to stock price) and C/P (ratio of cash flow per share to stock price) work much like the HML portfolio and hence reflect the same combination of the underlying common factors in returns. However, MMV proxies constructed from sales rank sort or from long term past return fails to replace L and H in tests of 3-factor model probably because they are not diversified enough. This diversifiable risk creates errors–in–variables problem that contaminates tests of three factor models.

A more serious problem facing the Fama and French model is its failure to explain the momentum effect of Jegadeesh and Titman (1993). Stocks that do well relative to the market over the last 3 to 12 months tend to continue to do well for the next few months and stocks that do poorly continue to do so. This momentum effect is distinct from the value effect captured by BE/ME equity and other price ratios. This momentum effect is left unexplained by both the three-factor model as well as the by the CAPM.

Following Carhart (1997) one response is to add a momentum factor (the difference between return on diversified portfolios of short-term winners and losers) to the three-factor model. This is reasonable in applications where the goal is to abstract from known patterns in average returns information specific or manager specific effects. But since the momentum effect is short lived it is largely irrelevant for estimation of the cost of equity capital.

3.7 ARBITRAGE PRICING THEORY

The CAPM has been one of the most popular models in finance and has a number of potentially useful applications in the areas of security pricing and portfolio management. However, it also suffers from some unwelcome assumptions and the concept of beta has not stood up in recent tests. There is also the problem that when an inflationary environment renders all real returns uncertain, the model in its simplest form cannot be subjected to a decisive test of validity.

In 1976 Ross presented an alternative more general model with a number of similarities to CAPM, which he called the 'Arbitrage Pricing Theory' (APT). The APT holds that a portfolio with no risk which mixes long and short positions in such a way that it requires no net investment of wealth, must earn zero return in a market with no transaction costs. In other words, the prices of stocks in a market should be such that it is not possible to make a profit by simply arbitraging between different stocks without making any net investment, or accepting any risk. If this were not the position, investors would quickly identify the opportunities to make pure profit and the resulting trading will cause the prices to adjust until these opportunities were eliminated.

The model begins with the assumption that the actual return realized in any security is equal to its expected return, plus a series of unexpected impacts on return, each of which is caused by some uncertain 'risk factor' (such as inflation), each multiplied by a coefficient that reflects the systematic degree of sensitivity of the stocks to that risk factor. Mathematically, this may be written as

$$R_i = E(R_i) + \beta_{i1} F_1 + \beta_{i2} F_2 + \ldots \beta_{iK} F_K + u_i \ldots\ldots\ldots(3.25)$$

where R_i is the realized return on security i, $E(R_i)$ is its expected return, β_{ij}, represents the sensitivity of the actual return on i to the jth risk factor (F_j) and u_i is a random 'white noise' that averages to zero.

By combining equation (3.25) with the condition that there should be no opportunities for pure arbitrage profits, Ross was able to derive the following expression for the expected return on a stock

$$E(R_i) = \alpha_0 + \beta_{i1} \alpha_1 + \beta_{i2} \alpha_2 + \ldots\ldots + \beta_{iK} \alpha_K \ldots\ldots(3.26)$$

where α's are the coefficients in the above regression.

If there is a riskless asset with a riskless rate of return R_f then β's are zero and $R_f = \alpha_0$, hence equation (3.26) can be rewritten as

$$E(R_i) - R_f = \beta_{i1} \alpha_1 + \beta_{i2} \alpha_2 + \ldots\ldots + \beta_{iK} \alpha_K \ldots\ldots\ldots(3.27)$$

The arbitrage pricing relationship (3.27) says that the arbitrage pricing relationship is linear and α represents the risk premium (i.e. the price of risk), in equilibrium for the kth factor.

Now rewriting equation (3.27) as

$$E(R_i) - R_f = \sum_{i=1}^{k} [\bar{\delta}_k - R_f] \beta \ldots\ldots\ldots(3.28)$$

where, $\bar{\delta}_K$ is the expected return on a portfolio with unit sensitivity to the kth factor and zero sensitivity to all other factors. Therefore, the risk premium α_k is equal to the difference between the expectations of a portfolio that has unit response to the kth factor and zero response to other factors and R_f. Thus, the APT model is represented by the following equation

$$E(R_i) - R_f = [\bar{\delta}_1 - R_f]\beta_{i1} + \cdots\cdots + [\bar{\delta}_k - R_f]\beta_{ik} \quad\cdots\cdots\cdots\cdots(3.29)$$

Equation (3.29) represents a linear regression equation and coefficients β_{ik} are defined in exactly the same way as beta in the CAPM.

A major problem in APT is that the factors affecting asset returns are unobservable. The conventional factor extraction techniques are maximum likelihood factor analysis and principle component approach. Since β_{ik} are not observable, we need to construct a proxy for the factor loadings. In factor analyses we can use estimated β as proxy then run a cross-section regression of R_i on β_{ik}.

3.8 EMPIRICAL ESTIMATION OF AN ASSET PRICING MODEL

3.8.1 Sampling Procedure

The study period covered was April 1999 to November 2004. The late 1990s and the early part of 2000 was marked by the dominance of Technology, Media and Telecom (TMT) stocks in stock markets world wide. A detailed analysis of the performance of TMT stocks during the sample period is, therefore, very important for modeling stock prices. By focusing on TMT stocks we can highlight the role of inertia in the Information-Technology (IT) boom that was prevalent in this period.

From the TMT stocks underlying the various BSE and NSE indices only 35 companies were found to have a continuous price data and information on economic fundamentals of the company for the period covered under the study. These, therefore, formed the sample for the present study. Monthly price data on the selected companies was obtained from the website of BSE. Various websites including those of BSE (www.bseindia.com), NSE (www.nseindia.com), India Infoline (www.indiainfoline.com) and Sify (www.sify.com) provided detailed information on the sample companies. Data on par value, number of shares issued, dividend rate, book-value, and earnings per share are thus collected from these sources. Market equity, to be used as a proxy for size is estimated as a product of the number of shares outstanding and price in the March of t (see Appendix A1). BE/ME ratio used for forming portfolios for year t are obtained by dividing the book value of the firm for the fiscal year ending in calendar year t-1 by the market equity at the end of December t-1. EPS/P is similarly obtained using EPS values recorded for the fiscal year ending in calendar year t-1 divided by the price in the December of t-1. The values of BE/ME and EPS/P of sample companies are given in Appendix A3 and A4. Monthly returns for all the stocks are calculated using the formula

$$R_{it} = \frac{P_{it} - P_{it-1} + D_{it}}{P_{it-1}} \dots\dots\dots\dots(3.30)$$

where P_{it}, P_{it-1} are prices in time period t and t-1 and

D_{it} is the dividend in time period t of stock i.

The BSE 500 Index is taken as a proxy for market portfolio and the value on this index is again collected from BSE website. Return on BSE Index is calculated as

$$R_{mt} = \frac{I_t - I_{t-1}}{I_{t-1}} \dots\dots\dots\dots(3.31)$$

From the above calculated R_{it} and R_{mt} we subtracted rate of interest as savings account to get r_{it} and r_{mt}, that is the excess return on stock i and BSE 500 index.

3.8.2 Portfolios at a glance

In general stock market studies are done using portfolios rather than stock returns. Holding a diversified portfolio is assumed to take care of firm specific risk. In this study portfolios were constructed using various criteria. Stocks were ranked on the basis of size, book-to-market value (BE/ME) and EPS/P and grouped to form portfolios. Over time as the order of rank changes, the composition of portfolio also changes. Both equal weighted and value weighted portfolios are constructed with the value weights being equal to the ratio of equity value of the firm to the aggregate total equity of all the sample firms (see Appendix A2). Beta sorted portfolios were constructed using stock level β of the financial year t-1 estimated by regressing excess return on stock on the excess market return i.e.

the following time-series regression is run

$$r_{it} = \hat{\alpha}_i + \hat{\beta}_i \hat{r}_{mt} + \varepsilon_{it}, \forall i \ \dots\dots(3.32)$$

The beta values for the various stocks obtained from the above regression are reported in Appendix A5. Portfolios were also constructed using cross-product of two ranking criteria. Thus, for instance, portfolios were constructed using both size - BE/ME criteria and also size -EPS/P ranking.

Table 3.8.1 shows the summary statistics of equal weighted portfolios. Portfolios 1 to 7 have each 5 stocks and are based on size criteria. Each portfolio consists of 5 stocks. Portfolio numbered 8 to 10 are based on BE/ME criteria, 17 to 19 on EPS/P ranking and 26 to 28 on beta ranking. In each of the above three cases each sub-group of low, medium and high consists of 12, 11, and 12 stocks. Stocks are also classified into two groups of small and big. This classification along with BE/ME and EPS/P ranking gives us the size-BE/ME (portfolios number 11 to 16) and size-EPS/P (portfolios number 20 to 25) sorted portfolios. Here SLBEME, for instance stands for Small and Low BE/ME category. Similarly SLEPS stands for Small and Low EPS/P category.

For each portfolio the following statistics are reported. (1) mean price; (2) standard deviation of price; (3) mean excess return on the portfolio; (4) standard deviation of the excess return on the portfolio; (5) portfolio beta; and (6) portfolio alpha. The last two statistics are obtained from the regression of excess portfolio returns on the excess market return. Column (7) indicates the size of the portfolio measured in terms of mean of the ME of the constituent firms. Mean of BE/ME and EPS/P ratios are given in column (8) and (9). The last column reports the 't'

value for the portfolio returns calculated as $t = \dfrac{\bar{r}}{S.D / \sqrt{66}}$. Here $\bar{r}$ and S.D refer to the mean and standard deviation of excess returns on portfolios.

Table 3.8.1. Summary Statistics

S.NO.	PORT	Price P		Ret		BETA	ALPHA	Mean			t
		MEAN	STD DEV	MEAN	STD DEV			ME	BE/ME	EPS/P	
1	Port1	45.686	55.1	0.1941	0.4816	0.9948	0.0946	1868.9	1.3746	0.6554	3.2722
2	Port2	98.876	161.07	0.0751	0.2232	1.0001	0.0628	7508.9	2.3402	-5E-04	2.7326
3	Port3	108.16	72.927	0.0516	0.2344	1.001	0.0476	19503	0.8236	0.436	1.7885
4	Port4	519.07	746.74	0.0483	0.2111	1.0021	0.0615	48549	1.0345	0.1899	1.8572
5	Port5	479.68	438.42	0.0144	0.1548	0.9985	-0.022	105644	0.5607	0.0717	0.7576
6	Port6	756.78	581.68	0.0225	0.1413	0.9985	-0.006	403314	0.6207	0.0911	1.293
7	Port7	1310.1	1137.4	0.0452	0.2323	0.9999	0.0338	3E+06	0.3634	0.0532	1.5795
8	Low	881.3	597.77	0.0202	0.1552	0.9996	-0.001	935077	0.0229	0.4838	1.0584
9	Medium	392.29	502.63	0.0675	0.1983	1.0011	0.073	420816	0.5644	0.0692	2.7639
10	High	141.76	120.07	0.1059	0.282	0.9972	0.0476	97406	2.4254	0.0765	3.05
11	SLBEME	156.36	241.53	0.0477	0.2156	0.9999	0.0214	9306.7	-0.197	1.2519	1.7946
12	SMBEME	161.29	202.64	0.0779	0.2267	1.0019	0.0942	13925	0.5331	0.0313	2.7924
13	SHBEME	78.308	75.039	0.1337	0.3641	0.997	0.0708	13143	2.8489	0.0587	2.9824
14	BLBEME	1227.6	943.78	0.0074	0.1597	0.9994	-0.013	1E+06	0.1382	0.0438	0.3752
15	BMBEME	547.73	684.87	0.0572	0.2064	1.0006	0.0549	793552	0.5848	0.0914	2.2521
16	BHBEME	266.7	224.67	0.04	0.1832	0.9979	-0.004	268539	1.5992	0.1132	1.7722

17	Low_E	679.56	724.02	0.0722	0.2971	0.9976	0.0195	945264	1.1969	-0.151	1.9726
18	Med_E	608.84	372.69	0.0411	0.1593	1.0012	0.047	395626	0.5245	0.0694	2.0959
19	High_E	145	109.45	0.0781	0.1758	0.9992	0.0509	104699	1.2881	0.7108	3.6098
20	SLEPS	101.79	107.4	0.1124	0.3121	1.0053	-0.045	11636	1.6745	-0.267	2.9258
21	SMEPS	329.34	475.65	0.0616	0.2765	1.0081	-0.037	15756	0.8146	0.0622	1.8097
22	SHEPS	78.596	94.901	0.0858	0.2069	1.007	-0.037	11786	1.3137	0.9519	3.3666
23	BLEPS	1053.7	970.29	0.0405	0.3672	1.0056	-0.093	2E+06	0.5983	0.0076	0.8961
24	BMEPS	786.06	713.76	0.032	0.1691	1.0084	-0.067	629717	0.4591	0.0695	1.5363
25	BHEPS	302.33	179.09	0.0592	0.1602	1.0048	-0.095	325581	1.0841	0.216	3.0022
26	Low(b)	471.41	450.92	0.0579	0.3273	1.0016	0.0141	577578	0.8277	0.1269	1.4367
27	Med(b)	673.75	682.15	0.0384	0.1739	1.002	0.0285	429521	0.9354	0.3163	1.7932
28	High(b)	293.65	345.88	0.0949	0.2737	1.003	0.0709	441016	1.2806	0.2069	2.8153

A study of the Table indicates that the dispersion in return is highest when stocks are classified into groups on the basis of size. Uniformity in return across portfolios is found when ranking is done on the basis of β and EPS/P. These two categories along with double-sort category of size-EPS/P do not conform unambiguously to the positive risk-return relationship where risk is measured in terms of standard deviation of returns.

Another interesting aspect highlighted by the table is that the 'β' value for all the portfolios is positive and close to 1, indicating a very strong co-movement between excess returns on constructed portfolios and the excess return on BSE_{500}. Further, less than half of the constructed portfolios seem to be worthwhile for investment purposes. This can be seen from the t values which show that only 13 out of 28 portfolios have a mean excess return significantly different from zero.

Also indicators like BE/ME, EPS/P which are commonly used by investors to evaluate the strength of the company give no clear cut directions for undertaking investment decisions. BE/ME and EPS/P for the sample companies seem to be very poorly correlated and their estimated coefficient is a meager 0.19.

3.8.3 Unit Root Test

It is now recognized that the time series of various variables of interest are non-stationary, i.e. they do not have constant mean and variance. Further, the covariance value depends upon the points at which covariance is measured. Under these circumstances classical techniques for inferences cannot be applied. Non-stationarity can be due to presence of unit root or time trend. The solutions for these call for difference stationary and trend stationary process, respectively. The number of times a series is differenced to achieve stationarity determines its degree of integration. With cointegration regression can be done in levels by identifying linear combinations which are stationary. Two series y_t and x_t are said to be co-integrated if:

1. both are integrated to the same order.
2. a linear combination of the two exists which is integrated to a lower order than the individual series.

Thus, if the long run relationship between y_t and x_t is given by

$$Y_t = bX_t + \varepsilon_t \quad \ldots\ldots\ldots(3.33)$$

where $\varepsilon_t \sim IN(0, \sigma^2)$ and so $\varepsilon_t \sim I(0)$.

If Y_t and X_t are I(1) the existence of co-integrating parameter b implies that the equilibrium error ε_t would be I(0) and would fluctuate around 0 as it has a zero mean. Whereas if Y_t and X_t were not co-integrated, then ε_t would fluctuate widely and it would rarely cross the zero line, suggesting that in this case the equilibrium concept has no significance.

The ADF test was done for all the thirty six constructed portfolios. The first six portfolios correspond to equal weighted and value weighted portfolios formed by using BE/ME criteria. The next twelve are equal and value weighted portfolios constructed using the size-BE/ME criteria. Similarly, the single sort EPS/P criteria generates a set of six portfolios formed using equal weights and value weights and the double sort size-EPS/P criteria produces two sets of equal weighted and value weighted portfolios each consisting of six sorts. The last three portfolios are factor portfolios used in the Fama and French three-factor model for explaining the returns process. The SMB portfolio is the difference, each month between the average of the returns on the three small stock portfolios (SLBEME, SMBEME, SHBEME) and the average of returns on the three big stock portfolios (BLMEME, BMBEME, BHBEME). HML is the difference between the average of the returns on the two high-BEME portfolios (SHBEME and BHBEME) and the average of returns on the two low-BEME portfolios (SLBEME and BLBEME). The last portfolio is the excess return on the portfolio underlying the BSE-500 index.

Table 3.8.2. Unit root test on returns on various portfolios.

Portfolio categories	ADF Test Statistic	Portfolio categories	ADF Test Statistic
LBEME	-4.39274	LEPSP	-4.50817
MBEME	-4.01194	MEPSP	-3.55762
HBEME	-4.59867	HEPSP	-3.7389
LBEME WTD	-5.18031	LEPSP WTD	-3.7908
MBEME WTD	-3.89775	MEPSP WTD	-4.24905
HBEME WTD	-4.4449	HEPSP WTD	-5.35248
SLBEME	-3.58284	SLEPS	-4.1587
SMBEME	-3.66651	SMEPS	-4.56958
SHBEME	-4.8988	SHEPS	-3.90226
BLBEME	-3.68762	BLEPS	-4.64291
BMBEME	-4.39183	BMEPS	-3.90823
BHBEME	-3.62454	BHEPS	-4.11845
SLBEME WTD	-4.26832	SLEPS WTD	-4.45268
SMBEME WTD	-3.84653	SMEPS WTD	-5.02462
SHBEME WTD	-4.66814	SHEPS WTD	-4.15495
BLBEME WTD	-3.95087	BLEPS WTD	-4.02282
BMBEME WTD	-3.69531	BMEPS WTD	-4.17855
BHBEME WTD	-3.52882	BHEPS WTD	-4.30645
		SMB	-4.72802
		HML	-4.97865
		EX RET B'SE	-4.02755

1% Critical Value *	-4.1059
5% Critical Value	-3.4801
10% Critical Value	-3.1675

A look at the graph of the portfolios returns series shows the absence of trend. Table 3.8.2 reports the results of unit root test on the portfolio returns. The ADF test on the above mentioned return series rejects the null of unit root at least at the 5% level of significance. For most (i.e twenty five out of the total of thirty nine), the test value exceeds even the 1% level of critical value. This result is to be expected as returns series are themselves differenced series.

3.8.4 Univariate regression (at the stock level)

The real world behavior of investors concentrating their wealth in a few selected stocks is a far cry from the assumption of investors holding a diversified portfolio. The latter is an abstraction used to derive a simplified risk-return relationship. A preliminary exercise is to understand the significance of each variable in explaining returns. The role of β, a variable which is often given the position of preeminence in the set of explanatory variable is looked at by regressing excess returns to each stock on its beta for each time period. For each t the cross-section regression

$$r_{it} = \delta_{0t} + \delta_{it} + \hat{\beta}_{it} + \upsilon_t \ldots\ldots \forall i = 1 \ldots N \quad \ldots\ldots\ldots(3.34)$$

is fitted by regressing the vector of excess returns on all 35 stocks over the vector of betas of all 35 stocks. The mean and standard deviation of estimated δ are used to calculate ` t' values .The calculated `t' values and the average R^2 are reported in Table 3.8.3.

Table 3.8.3. Monthly Regressions of Stock Returns on Beta, ME, BE/ME EPS/P, EPS/P neg, lnME,and lnB/M

The Univariate Regression

	BETA	ME	BE/ME	EPS/P	EPS/P neg	lnME	LnB/M
Mean	0.01104	-1.80E-08	0.01459	0.03510	0.01281	-0.01505	0.02344
StdDev	0.10164	0.00000	0.06711	0.16832	0.29377	0.03428	0.08537
T Val	0.88219	-2.45755	1.76487	1.69340	0.35402	-3.56501	2.22980
Avg R^2	(0.10678)	(0.03436)	(0.04934)	(0.046115)		(0.06538)	(0.06392)

The result shows positive but very insignificant relationship between stock returns and their betas. Similar univariate regressions are also run using BE/ME, ME, lnBE/ME and lnME. Here lnBE/ME and lnME refer to the natural log of BE/ME, ME. Both lnBE/ME and lnME have greater significance and better explanatory power than B/M and MV. In the case of EPS/P, since some companies report negative EPS values, we run the regression by bifurcating the EPS/P variable into two variables of EPS/P(positive) and EPS/P(negative). Both these variables (i.e. EPS/P(positive) and EPS/P(negative) are insignificant and have a very flat relationship with the stock returns. The average R^2 for each regression is the average overtime of R^2 value of cross-section regression. The low value of R^2 reflects the poor performance of all the variables.

3.8.5 Fama and French Three-Factor Model

Modeling asset prices requires estimation of expected returns. Fama and French (1993) developed a three-factor model for expected returns which includes apart from beta (the systematic risk component) two additional measures of risk related to size and book to market value. The expected excess return on any constructed portfolio i is given by equation (3.23).

Fama and French (1995) show that there is covariance in returns between firms grouped according to the BE/ME value, which is not captured by 'β'. In this model firms with high BE/ME value are treated as weak firms experiencing distress. The risk associated with such firms gets priced and is reflected in high returns and positive $\hat{h}_i$. On the other hand, firms with low BE/ME values are strong firms and have negative loading on $\hat{h}_i$.

Similarly, small firms have low earnings on assets and are less profitable than big firms. So size is treated as a proxy for risk factor and therefore small firms will have higher expected returns and positive slope on SMB as against big firms which have lower expected returns and negative slope SMB.

The model is estimated by running the regression

$$R_i - R_f = a_i + b_i(R_m - R_f) + S_I(SMB) + h_i(HML) + \varepsilon_i \quad \cdots (3.35)$$

and validated by testing for H0:α_i =0. We estimate this regression for the thirty-six portfolios, eighteen of which were constructed using BE/ME ranking and the other eighteen using EPS/P ranking. The construction of all these portfolios along with the factor portfolio of SMB and HML have already been described in earlier sections. The results for both the set of portfolios are given in Table 3.8.4 and Table 3.8.5

Table 3.8.4: Regression of excess returns to portfolios formed on the basis of BE/ME criteria on the Fama and French factor portfolios

Variable	Portfolio	C	EXRETBSE	SMB	HML
Coefficient	LBEME	0.0555	1.1438	0.2710	-0.2611
Std. Error	LBEME	0.0119	0.1168	0.0873	0.0394
t-Statistic	LBEME	4.6594	9.7965	3.1045	-6.6320
Prob.	LBEME	0.0000	0.0000	0.0029	0.0000
R^2: 0.729658, **Adj R^2**: 0.716785, **F Stat**: 56.67943, **Pr(F)**: 0, **DW stat**: 1.8561					
Coefficient	MBEME	0.0564	0.9606	0.6146	0.1557
Std. Error	MBEME	0.0203	0.1990	0.1488	0.0671
t-Statistic	MBEME	2.7744	4.8269	4.1310	2.3204
Prob.	MBEME	0.0073	0.0000	0.0001	0.0236
R^2 : 0.518473, **Adj. R^2** : 0.495543, **F-stat** : 22.61129, **Pr(F)** : 0, **DW stat** : 1.769499					
Coefficient	HBEME	0.0636	1.1971	0.6804	0.7235
Std. Error	HBEME	0.0127	0.1241 ·	0.0928	0.0418
t-Statistic	HBEME	5.0202	9.6478	7.3352	17.2948
Prob.	HBEME	0.0000	0.0000	0.0000	0.0000
R2 : 0.9069, **Adj.** R2 : 0.9024, **F-stat** : 204.4492, **Pr(F)** : 0, **DW stat** : 2.071352					
Coefficient	LBEME WTD	0.0410	1.1212	0.1356	-0.1073
Std. Error	LBEME WTD	0.0194	0.1903	0.1423	0.0642
t-Statistic	LBEME WTD	2.1125	5.8917	0.9534	-1.6717
Prob.	LBEME WTD	0.0386	0.0000	0.3440	0.0995
R^2 : 0.411505, **Adj. R^2** : 0.383481, **F-stat** : 14.68424, **Pr(F)** : 0, **DW stat** : 1.766371					
Coefficient	MBEME WTD	0.0649	0.6610	0.0684	-0.0799
Std. Error	MBEME WTD	0.0244	0.2386	0.1784	0.0805
t-Statistic	MBEME WTD	2.6656	2.7699	0.3833	-0.9928
Prob.	MBEME WTD	0.0098	0.0074	0.7028	0.3246
R^2 : 0.1371, **Adj. R^2** : 0.096009, **F-stat** : 3.336531, **Pr(F)** : 0.024845, **DW stat** : 2.239134					
Coefficient	HBEME WTD	0.0703	1.2469	0.0697	0.2597
Std. Error	HBEME WTD	0.0163	0.1598	0.1195	0.0539
t-Statistic	HBEME WTD	4.3078	7.8026	0.5834	4.8203
Prob.	HBEME WTD	0.0001	0.0000	0.5617	0.0000
R^2: 0.597289, **Adj. R^2** : 0.578113, **F-stat** : 31.14661, **Pr(F)** : 0,					

DW stat : 1.769802

Variable	Portfolio	C	EXRETBSE	SMB	HML
Coefficient	SLBEME	-0.0001	1.0817	1.0512	-0.3780
Std. Error		0.0150	0.1466	0.1096	0.0494
t-Statistic		-0.0087	7.3762	9.5893	-7.6457
Prob.		0.9931	0.0000	0.0000	0.0000

R^2 : 0.779528, **Adj. R^2** : 0.769029, **F-stat** : 74.25004, **Pr(F)** : 0,
DW stat : 2.200939

Variable	Portfolio	C	EXRETBSE	SMB	HML
Coefficient	SMBEME	0.0192	1.0582	0.9427	-0.0645
Std. Error		0.0225	0.2202	0.1646	0.0742
t-Statistic		0.8525	4.8059	5.7271	-0.8687
Prob.		0.3971	0.0000	0.0000	0.3883

R^2 : 0.546611, **Adj. R^2** : 0.525021, **F-stat** : 25.31784, **Pr(F)** : 0,
DW stat : 1.445583

Variable	Portfolio	C	EXRETBSE	SMB	HML
Coefficient	SHBEME	0.0128	1.1199	1.0449	0.9460
Std. Error		0.0165	0.1618	0.1209	0.0545
t-Statistic		0.7781	6.9225	8.6397	17.3435
Prob.		0.4394	0.0000	0.0000	0.0000

R^2 : 0.905712, **Adj. R^2** : 0.901222, **F-stat** : 201.7219, **Pr(F)** : 0,
DW stat : 2.227075

Variable	Portfolio	C	EXRETBSE	SMB	HML
Coefficient	BLBEME	0.0191	1.1927	-0.1488	-0.2284
Std. Error		0.0145	0.1419	0.1061	0.0478
t-Statistic		1.3222	8.4063	-1.4029	-4.7737
Prob.		0.1909	0.0000	0.1656	0.0000

R^2 : 0.625001, **Adj. R^2** : 0.607144, **F-stat** : 35.00012, **Pr(F)** : 0,
DW stat : 1.700596

Variable	Portfolio	C	EXRETBSE	SMB	HML
Coefficient	BMBEME	0.0066	0.9127	0.3300	0.2842
Std. Error		0.0232	0.2271	0.1697	0.0766
t-Statistic		0.2832	4.0196	1.9443	3.7124
Prob.		0.7779	0.0002	0.0563	0.0004

R^2 : 0.418922, **Adj. R^2** : 0.391251, **F-stat** : 15.13971, **Pr(F)** : 0,
DW stat : 2.1534

Variable	Portfolio	C	EXRETBSE	SMB	HML
Coefficient	BHBEME	0.0062	1.1544	-0.1425	0.4476
Std. Error		0.0135	0.1321	0.0988	0.0446
t-Statistic		0.4573	8.7359	-1.4424	10.0475
Prob.		0.6490	0.0000	0.1542	0.0000

R^2 : 0.734162, **Adj. R^2** : 0.721503, **F-stat** : 57.99538, **Pr(F)** : 0,
DW stat : 1.493536

Variable	Portfolio	C	EXRETBSE	SMB	HML
Coefficient	SLBEME WTD	0.0498	1.1756	0.8519	-0.2992
Std. Error		0.0197	0.1928	0.1441	0.0650
t-Statistic		2.5320	6.0977	5.9110	-4.6034
Prob.		0.0138	0.0000	0.0000	0.0000

R^2 : 0.629524, **Adj. R^2** : 0.611883, **F-stat** : 35.68388, **Pr(F)** : 0,
DW stat : 1.580422

Variable	Portfolio	C	EXRETBSE	SMB	HML
Coefficient	SMBEME WTD	0.0684	1.1905	1.2132	-0.0955
Std. Error		0.0374	0.3663	0.2738	0.1235
t-Statistic		1.8289	3.2503	4.4311	-0.7734
Prob.		0.0721	0.0019	0.0000	0.4422

R^2 : 0.392514, **Adj. R^2** : 0.363586, **F-stat** : 13.56868, **Pr(F)** : 0.000001,
DW stat : 1.586517

Variable	Portfolio	C	EXRETBSE	SMB	HML
Coefficient	SHBEME WTD	0.0878	2.1221	0.7963	0.0389
Std. Error		0.0352	0.3446	0.2576	0.1162
t-Statistic		2.4951	6.1575	3.0908	0.3350
Prob.		0.0152	0.0000	0.0030	0.7388
R^2 : 0.499521, **Adj. R^2** : 0.475688, **F-stat** : 20.95978, **Pr(F)** : 0, **DW stat** : 1.86278					
Coefficient	BLBEME WTD	0.0802	1.2069	0.0551	-0.3459
Std. Error		0.0203	0.1987	0.1485	0.0670
t-Statistic		3.9560	6.0745	0.3710	-5.1645
Prob.		0.0002	0.0000	0.7119	0.0000
R^2 : 0.532376, **Adj. R^2** : 0.510108, **F-stat** : 23.90784, **Pr(F)** : 0, **DW stat** : 1.527014					
Coefficient	BHBEME WTD	0.0578	1.0939	-0.1367	0.1659
Std. Error		0.0174	0.1701	0.1271	0.0573
t-Statistic		3.3289	6.4316	-1.0751	2.8941
Prob.		0.0015	0.0000	0.2864	0.0052
R^2 : 0.431952, **Adj. R^2** : 0.404903, **F-stat** : 15.96874, **Pr(F)** : 0, **DW stat** : 1.873639					

(i) For the six equal weighted size-BE/ME portfolios, the H0: $\alpha_i = 0$ is accepted. The null, however, does not hold for value weighted size-BE/ME (except SMBEME) as also for single sort BE/ME (both equal and value weighted) portfolios evaluated at 5% level of significance.

(ii) As compared to value weighted portfolios, equal weighted portfolios seem to have both better explanatory power, as also greater sensitivity to size and BE/ME factors.

(iii) Slope on SMB is high and strong in the small category for both equal and value weighted portfolios. In the big group SMB is not only small in magnitude but also insignificant. Also, the slope coefficient is positively related to returns in some categories. Similarly when ranking is on the basis of BE/ME alone, SMB is significant for equal weighted category and not for value weighted category.

(iv) Loadings on HML on all the portfolios is strongly supported in all except SMBEME (both equal and value weighted) and SHBEME value weighted stocks. In all the regressions low BE/ME stocks have negative coefficients whereas high BE/ME stocks have positive coefficients.

(v) The explanatory power of regression is good when the BE/ME criteria is used alone for constructing portfolios. Combined with size the regression works well for small as against big. Equal weighted portfolios seem to do better than value weighted.

All these facts imply that whereas the model picks up the premium associated with small size when in the first place small size is already highlighted, it fails to establish a discount in returns for big sized firms. It however, prices the risk captured by BE/ME factor along the predicted lines of the model.

EPS/P Criteria

The regression estimates of equation 3.35 using portfolios constructed on the basis of EPS/P ranking also shows poor performance of the multifactor model.

Table 3.8.5: Regression of excess returns to portfolios formed on the basis of EPS/P ranking on the Fama and French factor portfolios

Variable	Portfolio	C	EXRETBSE	SMB	HML
Coefficient		0.07356	0.27303	0.12577	0.05429
Std. Error	LEPS	0.04371	0.42696	0.32097	0.14482
t-Statistic		1.68276	0.63946	0.39183	0.37484
Prob.		0.09750	0.52490	0.69650	0.70910

R^2 : 0.015936, **Adj. R^2** : -0.031681, **F-stat** : 0.334667, **Pr(F)** : 0.800302, **DW stat** : 1.959073

Variable	Portfolio	C	EXRETBSE	SMB	HML
Coefficient		0.04847	0.28651	-0.02795	0.11045
Std. Error	MEPS	0.02281	0.22281	0.16750	0.07558
t-Statistic		2.12505	1.28591	-0.16684	1.46150
Prob.		0.03760	0.20330	0.86800	0.14890

R^2 : 0.057557, **Adj. R^2** : 0.011955, **F-stat** : 1.262166, **Pr(F)** : 0.295171, **DW stat** : 1.513409

Variable	Portfolio	C	EXRETBSE	SMB	HML
Coefficient		0.08292	0.35006	0.06203	0.08726
Std. Error	HEPS	0.02496	0.24383	0.18330	0.08271
t-Statistic		3.32174	1.43567	0.33839	1.05501
Prob.		0.00150	0.15610	0.73620	0.29550

R^2 : 0.060813, **Adj. R^2**: 0.015369, **F-stat** : 1.33819, **Pr(F)** : 0.270128, **DW stat** : 1.574677

Variable	Portfolio	C	EXRETBSE	SMB	HML
Coefficient		0.01222	0.93826	0.21443	0.31796
Std. Error	LEPS WTD	0.03066	0.30042	0.22458	0.10129
t-Statistic		0.39842	3.12317	0.95480	3.13916
Prob.		0.69170	0.00270	0.34330	0.00260

R^2 : 0.288691, **Adj. R^2** : 0.254819, **F-stat** : 8.523022, **Pr(F)** : 0.000078, **DW stat** : 2.011206

Variable	Portfolio	C	EXRETBSE	SMB	HML
Coefficient		0.05450	0.99187	0.14847	-0.12589
Std. Error	MEPS WTD	0.01717	0.16824	0.12577	0.05672
t-Statistic		3.17350	5.89561	1.18054	-2.21936
Prob.		0.00230	0.00000	0.24220	0.03010

R^2 : 0.428757, **Adj. R^2**: 0.401555, **F-stat** : 15.76191, **Pr(F)** : 0, **DW stat** : 1.684436

Variable	Portfolio	C	EXRETBSE	SMB	HML
Coefficient		0.09332	1.11614	0.02944	0.15345
Std. Error	HEPS WTD	0.02028	0.19870	0.14853	0.06699
t-Statistic		4.60121	5.61732	0.19819	2.29066
Prob.		0.00000	0.00000	0.84350	0.02530

R^2 : 0.386993, **Adj. R^2**: 0.357803, **F-stat** : 13.25738, **Pr(F)** : 0.000001, **DW stat** : 2.00087

Variable	Portfolio	C	EXRETBSE	SMB	HML
Coefficient	SLEPS	0.04856	1.01958	1.24159	0.52270

Variable	Portfolio	C	EXRETBSE	SMB	HML
Std. Error		0.02286	0.22400	0.16745	0.07552
t-Statistic		2.12410	4.55175	7.41474	6.92129
Prob.		0.03760	0.00000	0.00000	0.00000
R^2 : 0.753754, **Adj. R^2**: 0.742028, **F-stat** : 64.28048, **Pr(F)** : 0, **DW stat** : 1.485309					
Coefficient		0.02634	1.20112	0.93722	0.39689
Std. Error	SMEPS	0.02362	0.23136	0.17295	0.07800
t-Statistic		1.11536	5.19152	5.41891	5.08808
Prob.		0.26890	0.00000	0.00000	0.00000
R^2 : 0.665265, **Adj. R^2**: 0.649326, **F-stat**: 41.73625, **Pr(F)** : 0, **DW stat** : 1.540788					
Coefficient		0.08589	1.30115	0.87156	-0.13619
Std. Error	SHEPS	0.01575	0.15429	0.11534	0.05202
t-Statistic		5.45437	8.43335	7.55677	-2.61807
Prob.		0.00000	0.00000	0.00000	0.01110
R^2 : 0.733367, **Adj. R^2**: 0.72067, **F-stat** : 57.75999, **Pr(F)** : 0, **DW stat** : 1.672131					
Coefficient		-0.01093	0.68180	0.26335	1.01195
Std. Error	BLEPS	0.03226	0.31604	0.23625	0.10655
t-Statistic		-0.33897	2.15735	1.11471	9.49716
Prob.		0.73580	0.03480	0.26920	0.00000
R^2 : 0.64529, **Adj. R^2**: 0.628399, **F-stat** : 38.20333, **Pr(F)** : 0, **DW stat** : 2.096983					

Variable	Portfolio	C	EXRETBSE	SMB	HML
Coefficient		0.07500	1.13054	0.10757	-0.24255
Std. Error	BMEPS	0.01687	0.16523	0.12352	0.05571
t-Statistic		4.44715	6.84209	0.87087	-4.35382
Prob.		0.00000	0.00000	0.38710	0.00010
R^2 : 0.543522, **Adj. R^2**: 0.521785, **F-stat** : 25.00439, **Pr(F)** : 0, **DW stat** : 1.527399					
Coefficient		0.10299	1.28214	-0.27650	0.15002
Std. Error	BHEPS	0.01640	0.16068	0.12012	0.05418
t-Statistic		6.27961	7.97922	-2.30186	2.76912
Prob.		0.00000	0.00000	0.02470	0.00740
R^2 : 0.516457, **Adj. R^2**: 0.493431, **F-stat**: 22.42944, **Pr(F)** : 0, **DW stat** : 1.738433					
Coefficient		0.00596	0.56734	0.82775	0.10171
Std. Error	SLEPS WTD	0.03591	0.35184	0.26301	0.11862
t-Statistic		0.16589	1.61251	3.14718	0.85742
Prob.		0.86880	0.11180	0.00250	0.39450
R^2 : 0.239598, **Adj. R^2**: 0.203389, **F-stat** : 6.616985, **Pr(F)** : 0.000588, **DW stat** : 2.106546					

Variable	Portfolio	C	EXRETBSE	SMB	HML

Variable	Portfolio	C		SMB	HML
Coefficient	SMEPS WTD	-0.00503	0.81910	1.23660	1.43760
Std. Error		0.04330	0.42423	0.31713	0.14303
t-Statistic		-0.11607	1.93079	3.89933	10.05105
Prob.		0.90800	0.05800	0.00020	0.00000

R^2 : 0.723983, **Adj. R^2**: 0.710839,   F-stat : 55.08229, **Pr(F)** : 0, **DW stat** : 1.81837

Variable	Portfolio	C		SMB	HML
Coefficient	SHEPS WTD	0.09074	1.33094	0.81333	-0.10569
Std. Error		0.02095	0.20530	0.15347	0.06922
t-Statistic		4.33055	6.48297	5.29963	-1.52688
Prob.		0.00010	0.00000	0.00000	0.13180

R^2 : 0.599555, **Adj. R^2**: 0.580487, **F-stat** : 31.44171, **Pr(F)** : 0, **DW stat** : 1.973558

Variable	Portfolio	C		SMB	HML
Coefficient	BLEPS WTD	0.00213	0.75395	0.17211	0.35835
Std. Error		0.03794	0.37168	0.27785	0.12531
t-Statistic		0.05602	2.02848	0.61942	2.85961
Prob.		0.95550	0.04670	0.53790	0.00570

R^2 : 0.197634, **Adj. R^2**: 0.159426, **F-stat** : 5.172583, **Pr(F)** : 0.002933, **DW stat** : 2.075304

Variable	**Portfolio**	**C**	**EXRETBSE**	**SMB**	**HML**
Coefficient	BMEPS WTD	0.05464	0.98493	0.12132	-0.14546
Std. Error		0.01772	0.17357	0.12975	0.05852
t-Statistic		3.08444	5.67459	0.93504	-2.48568
Prob.		0.00300	0.00000	0.35330	0.01560

R^2 : 0.415184, **Adj. R^2**: 0.387336, **F-stat**: 14.90876, **Pr(F)** : 0, **DW stat** : 1.654545

Variable	Portfolio	C	EXRETBSE	SMB	HML
Coefficient	BHEPS WTD	0.09011	0.99179	-0.22296	0.12052
Std. Error		0.01574	0.15423	0.11530	0.05200
t-Statistic		5.72397	6.43046	-1.93381	2.31776
Prob.		0.00000	0.00000	0.05760	0.02370

R^2 : 0.410892, **Adj. R^2**: 0.38284, **F-stat** : 14.64714, **Pr(F)** : 0, **DW stat** : 2.477247

In both equal and value weighted double sort category for only 3 out of 6 portfolios, the three-factor model fails to reject the H_0. In the single sort category again for only portfolios LEPS and LEPS weighted the H_0 is not rejected again evaluated at 5% level of significance.

(i) The slope coefficients on SMB and HML also do not conform to the three-factor model. None of the low EPS/P portfolios have a negative loading on HML. Similarly in the big size-EPS/P category none have significant SMB and only 2 out of 6 big-size portfolios have negative coefficient on SMB.

(ii) In addition to reporting univariate statistic for each equation, we adopt a systems approach to simultaneous testing of all intercepts equal to zero. Following Gibbons et al. (1989), we estimate a statistic

$$W = \frac{\hat{\alpha}'\hat{\Sigma}^{-1}\hat{\alpha}}{(1+\bar{\mu}'\hat{\Omega}\bar{\mu})} \quad \ldots\ldots\ldots\ldots\ldots(3.36)$$

The test statistic $\dfrac{T(T-N-L)}{N(T-L-1)} * W \sim F(N, T-N-L)$

where N = 1…35, T = 1….67,

$\hat{\alpha}$ = is the vector of intercept of all the portfolios

$\hat{\Sigma}$ = is the unbiased residual covariance matrix.

$\bar{\mu}$ is a vector of sample means of excess return on BSE, SMB, HML.

$\hat{\Omega}$ is the unbiased estimate of the covariance matrix of factors.

And L is the number of factor portfolios considered. In the present case, therefore, L is equal to three.

The values of $\hat{\alpha}'\hat{\Sigma}^{-1}\hat{\alpha}$, $\dfrac{T(T-N-3)}{N(T-4)} * W$ and the associated p values are given in Table 3.8.6.

This multivariate test was done on each category separately. The first set has equal weighted portfolios based on BE/ME classification. So this set is a system of three equations. The second set consists of three value weighted portfolios based on BE/ME ranking. Similarly the third and fourth set each have six portfolios based on size-BE/ME classification constructed using equal weights and value weights. The last four categories pertains to similar sets formed using EPS/P classification. The last three rows of the table gives us the mean return on the three factor portfolios.

Table 3.8.6. A multivariate approach to categorywise regression of excess returns on the Fama and French factor portfolios.

PORTFOLIO CATEGORIES	$\hat{\alpha}' \sum^{-1} \hat{\alpha}$	$\dfrac{T(T-N-3)}{N(T-4)} * W$	$P*$
BE/ME	5.34E-05	4.38E-06	1
BE/Mewtd	0.000373	0.000306	1
SBE/ME	3.74E-05	3.07E-06	1
SBE/Mewtd	0.0009	0.000822	1
EPS	0.001241	0.001018	1
EPSwtd	0.000225	0.000185	1
SEPS	0.000138	0.000113	1
SEPSwtd	0.000403	0.00033	1
mean of ert on BSE	-0.03053		
mean of SMB	0.052425		
mean of HML	0.055789		

*P values are the 'F' probability distribution at 1% obtained using the FDIST function of Excel.

As can be seen the multivariate test fails to reject the null for all the portfolio categories. As noted the Gibbons et al. statistic is influenced by the number of portfolios in each category. Hence this failure may be low due to low power of the test to detect deviation from the null hypothesis.

3.9 CONCLUSIONS

The results of univariate regression and Fama and French model challenges us with a need to develop alternate model for describing the stock market behavior in the late 1990s and early 2000. The rise in stock prices not justified by fundamentals directs us into the realm of behavioral inertia. In behavioral inertia approach we directly model stock prices rather than pass through the intermediate stage of estimating E(R). By building a model which incorporates behavioral biases of investors, we hope to provide a better description of stock price formation.

CHAPTER 4: BEHAVIORAL PRINCIPLES OF STOCK MARKET

In this chapter the psychological underpinnings of investor behavior are analyzed. The neoclassical approach with its emphasis on rationality and utility maximization on the part of individuals has great theoretical appeal but little practical relevance. **Section 4.1** of this chapter notes the drawbacks of neoclassical approach. Although, starting from Adam Smith, economists were always aware of the influence of psychological principles on human behavior, serious attempts to incorporate behavioral biases in economic analysis occurred much later. In **Section 4.2** the emergence of discipline of behavioral economics as a realistic approach to solving economic problems is discussed.

In an uncertain world, individuals operate under various resource constraints. A natural outcome of this situation is the use of various rules of thumb to arrive at decisions. In **Section 4.3** we elaborate on the various judgment and decision biases the investors are prone to. In **Section 4.4** we look at the behavioral school's interpretation of the anomalies on CAPM and the efficient market hypothesis-the two pillars of modern finance. We report on the literature that uses psychological realism to study asset market behavior.

Inertia plays a stabilizing role in regulating an investor's behavior. The stock prices are influenced by a large number of macro level and firm level factors. Keeping track of such information changes is impossible for investor's with limited amount of time and money at their disposal. We develop a behavioral model which incorporates inertia as the guiding force. This is done in **Section 4.5** and its empirical validation is done in the **Section 4.6**.

4.1 DRAWBACKS OF NEOCLASSICAL APPROACH

The neoclassical approach to economics is based on the concepts of utility maximization, equilibrium and efficiency. The neoclassical approach has been popular because it enables economists to develop a neat theoretical framework to study and test various forms of economics behavior. This approach, however, imposes stringent assumption on the behavior of economic agents. The assumption of perfect rationality, for example, has come in for a lot of criticism. It is now recognized that individuals at best have imperfect rationality. Herbert Simon (1955) suggested the term 'bounded rationality' to describe a more realistic conception of human problem solving capabilities. With limited time and brainpower, individuals cannot be expected to solve difficult problems optimally.

Similarly, the restrictive assumption of maximizing behavior of economic agents has to be replaced by the realistic alternative of 'satisfying behavior' on the part of the individuals faced with cognitive limitations and bounded rationality.

An assumption that is found to be useful in optimization exercises is that having solved for the optimum, individuals choose the optimum. Again this may not be so. Individuals, even when they know what is best, sometimes fail to choose it for self-control reasons. Similarly, the assumption that people are always guided by self-interest is not completely true. People often take selfless actions, do charity and volunteer work.

With these modified assumptions it is no longer certain that equilibrium values would be achieved. In the capital market, for instance, while the trading by rational traders traces the path towards equilibrium, trading activities of irrational traders pushes the market away from the equilibrium point. The equilibrium prices are a weighted average of the beliefs of rational and irrational traders, and the influence of either group on prices depends upon their risk bearing capacity. Arbitrage will, therefore, not eliminate mispricing. Arbitraging does not work efficiently, since it is hard for an investor to know whether other investors have yet detected and acted upon it.

Persistent mispricing might also occur because some relevant piece of public information is either ignored or misused by everyone leading to market prices being regularly at odds with fundamental values. To argue that errors are independent across individuals and will cancel out in equilibrium is also not correct, as individuals have similar biases. Neoclassical economists arguing for the existence of equilibrium held that individuals who systematically and consistently make the same mistake, will eventually learn the error of their ways. However, experimentation literature has shown that there can be a complete lack of learning even in infinite horizons. Since there are some opportunity costs to learning, even a completely 'rational' learner will chose not to experiment and remain in a non-optimal equilibrium, simply because the cost of trying something else is too high. Moreover, the time required to converge to an equilibrium strategy can be extremely long, especially in a situation of changing environment. Thus, markets can be in a situation of perpetual non-convergence.

4.2 EMERGENCE OF BEHAVIORAL ECONOMICS

Paradoxically, the origins of behavioral economics can be traced to the roots of neoclassical economics, the very same field to which it is trying to provide a realistic alternative. As psychology did not gain the status of a distinct field of study for quite some time, most of the research on human behavior was done by the economists of that time. Adam Smith, for instance, wrote a book 'The theory of moral sentiments' which laid out psychological principles of individual behavior. The book gives us insight about human psychology, many of which presage current developments in behavioral economics. Jeremy Bentham, whose utility concept formed the foundation of neoclassical economics, wrote extensively about the psychological underpinnings of utility.

At the turn of the twentieth century, hoping to cast economics in the mould of a natural science, many economists raised their voice against using psychology in the field of economics. In the early part of the twentieth century, the writings of economists such as Fisher and Pareto still included rich speculations about how people feel and think about economic choices. Later, Keynes very much appealed to psychological insights but by the middle of the century discussions on psychology had largely disappeared.

Throughout the second half of the century many criticisms of the positivistic perspective took place in both economics and psychology. In economics, researchers like Harvey Leibenstein, Tibor Scitovsky and Herbert Simon wrote books and articles suggesting the importance of psychological measures and bounds on rationality. These commentaries attracted a lot of attention, but were unable to alter the fundamental directions of economics.

Many coincident developments led to the emergence of behavioral economics as a distinct field of study. One development was the rapid acceptance by economists of the expected utility and discounted utility models as normative and descriptive models of decision making under uncertainty and inter-temporal choice, respectively. Whereas, the assumption and implications of generic utility analysis are rather flexible and hence tricky to refute, the expected utility and discounted utility models have numerous precise and testable implications. As a result, they provided some of the first areas of research for critics of the standard theory. Seminal papers of Ellsberg (1961) and Markowitz (1952) pointed out anomalous implications of expected and subjective expected utility. Strotz (1955) questioned exponential discounting. Later, scientists demonstrated similar anomalies using compelling experiments that were easy to replicate (Kahneman and Tversky 1979 on expected utility and Thaler 1981 and Lowenstein and Prelec 1992 on discounted utility).

As soon as economists realized that anomalies can be explained by using principles falling outside the realm of economics, they sought in psychology, directions to explain these anomalies. Beginning around 1960, cognitive psychology became dominated by the metaphor of the brain as an information processing devise replacing the behaviorist conception of the brain as a stimulus-response machine. The information processing metaphor permitted a fresh study of neglected topics like memory, problem solving and decision making. These new topics were more relevant to the neo-classical conception of utility maximization than behaviorism had appeared to be. Psychologists such as Ward Edwards, Duncan Lee, Amos Tversky and Daniel Kahneman, began to use economic models as a benchmark against which to contrast their psychological models. Perhaps the two most influential contributions were reported by Tversky and Kahneman. Their 1974 article published in the journal 'Science', argued that heuristic shortcuts created probability judgments which deviated from statistical principles. Their 1979 paper, 'Prospect theory: decision making under risk' documented violations of expected utility and proposed an axiomatic theory grounded in psychological principles to explain the violations. By mid-1980s, the discipline started attracting a lot of attention from social scientists. A final recognition came in the form of award of the Nobel Prize for economics in 2002 to David Kahneman and Amos Tversky for their research on judgment and heuristics.

4.3 BIASES IN BELIEFS AND CHOICE

All individuals have biases especially under conditions when information is slack. While it might be argued that in the modern day computerized world, information is no longer a constraint, the question of quality of information, its proper interpretation and analyses still remains.

A direct outcome of cognitive resource constraints is the use of heuristics to make decisions. In their interaction with other fellow beings, people often try to draw conclusions by reading the body language of others. Bias arises as individuals have exaggerated beliefs regarding their attributes. More often than not, actions are guided by emotions that overpower reasoning and leads to a third source of bias in decision making. Hirshleifer (2001) argued that, a) heuristic simplification, b) self deception and c) emotional loss of control provide a unified explanation for most known judgment and decision biases.

4.3.1 Heuristic simplification

Time constraint, limited memory and finite processing capacities force individuals to focus on subsets of available information. They, therefore, under-weigh the probabilities of contingencies that are not explicitly available for consideration. This results in overconfidence and apparent market over-reaction when unforeseen contingencies do occur.

One way of overcoming such limitations is habit formation, considered as a response to a certain kind of stimulus. As it gets repeated, it generates inertia in behavior. Similarly, the tendency to generalize a particular characteristic leads to the 'halo-effect'. Thus, if people mistakenly extend their favorable evaluation of a stock's earnings prospects to its return prospects, growth stocks will be overpriced.

There are ease of processing effects analogous to the effects of ease of retrieval. People are more comfortable accepting statements that are easy to process. Decisions involving familiar things are also perceived to be less risky.

Herd behavior explains why people tend to imitate others. When a market is moving up or down, investors are subject to a fear that others know more or have more information. As a consequence, investors feel a strong impulse to do what others are doing. They also place too much worth on judgments derived from small samples of date or from single sources. For instance, investors are known to attribute skill rather than luck to an analyst who picks a winning stock.

A central tenet of behavioral choice theory holds that decisions are influenced by how choices are framed. Considerable evidence derived from controlled experiments supports this claim and suggested other systematic derivation from expected utility maximization. These findings provided the foundation for Kahneman and Tversky's (1979) formulation of prospect theory. Prospect theory asserts that individuals make choices under uncertainty by maximizing a value function that evaluates wealth changes rather than expected utility function that ranks choices according to the level of expected utility. The value function is positive and concave in the domain of positive changes and negative and convex in the domain of negative changes.

Ljungqvist and Wilhelm Jr. (2005) used prospect theory to derive a behavioral measure of the IPO decision maker's satisfaction with the underwriter's performance and evaluated its ability to explain the decision maker's choice among underwriters in subsequent securities offerings. The decision maker's initial valuation belief (reflected in the mean of the indicative price range reported in the issuing firm's IPO registration statement) is treated as a reference point against which the gain or loss from the outcome of an IPO is assessed. The authors found that though the behavioral model has explanatory power, it does not explain whether deviation from expected utility maximization determines patterns in IPO initial return.

Narrow framing or analyzing problem in too isolated a fashion is also resorted to when time and cognitive resources are limited. The presentation of a problem and the choice of a reference point can significantly influence decision. Many experimenters have shown that by using different presentations or procedures, preference reversals can easily be elicited from the subjects.

Mental accounting (Thaler, 1985) is a kind of narrow framing where profit and loss making decisions are compartmentalized into separate mental accounts. This viewpoint explains the disposition effect of Shefrin and Statman (1985), that investors are less willing to sell a loser than a winner even when the tax law encourages just the opposite behavior. This probably is a confirmation of the working of self-deception theory, which holds that realizing losses reduces the self-esteem of investors and therefore, they deceive themselves by holding on to securities that have declined in value.

Coval and Shumway (2005) have recently documented how a high level of loss-aversion gives rise to behavioral biases among traders. They reported that Chicago board of proprietary traders assume above average afternoon risk to recover from morning losses. This behavior has important short-term consequences for afternoon prices, as losing traders actively purchase contracts at higher prices and sell contracts at lower prices than those that prevailed previously. Interestingly, however, the market seemed to distinguish these risk-seeking trades from informed trades. Prices set by loss-averse traders are reversed significantly more quickly than those set by unbiased traders.

Regret avoidance also reflects a self-deception mechanism designed to protect self esteem about decision making ability (Joseph et al. 1996). Kahneman and Tversky (1982) showed that regret is stronger for decisions that involve action rather than inaction. Regret aversion explains the endowment effect, a preference for people to hold on to what they have rather than exchange for a better alternative.

The representativeness heuristic involves assessing the probability of a state of the world based on the degree to which the evidence is perceived as similar to or typical of the state of the world (Kahneman and Tversky 1973, Tversky and Kahneman 1974 and Grether 1980). However, this perception of a piece of evidence being representative of a state of world may not match its conditional probability. More importantly, use of representativeness heuristic causes trend chasing because people are ready to believe that trends have systematic causes.

Hirshleifer and Welch (2000) argued that individuals faced with memory loss are able to recall their actions better than the information on the basis of which such an action was undertaken. They developed a model to show whether individuals exhibit inertia or impulsiveness in the face of new information. They found that if past actions were highly informative a player will optimally exhibit excess inertia; if past actions were less informative the player may optimally exhibit excess impulsiveness; and if past actions were very uninformative there would be neither inertia nor impulsiveness.

4.3.2 Self-deception

This implies overconfidence. People in general, believe their knowledge to be more accurate than it really is. While success in decision making is attributed to their abilities, failures are treated as an outcome of external factors. This is recognized as biased self attribution. Overconfidence and biased self-attribution are static and dynamic counterparts; self attribution causes individuals to learn to be overconfident rather than converging to an accurate self-assessment.

4.3.3 Emotions

Many a times individuals' actions are guided by emotions. Mann (1992) discussed how mood and emotions affect people's perceptions of and choices with respect to risk. In general, people who are in good moods are more optimistic in their choices and judgments than those in bad moods (e.g. Wright & Bower 1992). However, people often attribute feelings to the wrong source, leading to incorrect judgments or misattribution biases (Ross 1977).

4.4 BEHAVIORAL APPROACH TO THE STUDY OF CAPITAL MARKET

Developments in behavioral approach to study the subject matter of finance have attacked the three basic tenets of corporate finance, namely, (i) rational behavior, (ii) CAPM, and (iii) efficient markets.

4.4.1 Rationality

Behavioral economists maintain that psychological factors impart bounded rationality on decision makers. They show that market prices are regularly at odds with fundamental value and security risk premiums are not fully determined by security betas.

Keynes (1936) highlighted investor irrationality when he talked of how valuations of stocks is carried out in practice, given that investors are generally unable to calculate numerical probabilities of possible outcomes of their investment decisions. In the Keynesian model, investors accept current valuations as a correct reflection of the market assessment of future prospects. They downplay the fact that these valuations are unlikely to be correct. They ignore the impact of factors they know nothing about and concentrate only on possible 'changes in the news' that might affect prices. By conscious mimetic behavior, market participants attempt to cope with the fact that they do not have a clear idea of what the future holds by endeavoring to conform to the behavior of the majority on the average.

However, this attempt to conform with the majority may itself be destabilizing of ruling valuations. In particular, the liquidity provided by asset market allows market participants to concern themselves, not with attempting to judge the probable long term yield of an investment, but with attempting to profit from predicting 'changes in the conventional basis of valuation a short time ahead of the general public'. Where speculative behavior of this kind becomes predominant, stock market prices may be driven from the levels associated from the existing conventions (which may or may not correspond to the objectively warranted 'fundamental' values) .

Thus, what is irrational at the individual level becomes conventional and realistic in the Keynesian analyses. The possibility therefore arises, for the stock market to be subjected to waves of optimistic or pessimistic sentiments, when no solid basis exists for such sentiment and movements in stock prices are caused largely by changes in the perception of ignorant speculators.

Using volatility tests to test the rationality of market behavior, Shiller (1981) found fluctuations in actual prices to be much greater than those implied by changes in fundamental variables. This was inferred as being the result of fads or waves of optimistic or pessimistic market psychology. The results of excess volatility in stock markets have been confirmed by many others. In a latter study Shiller (1991) investigated investors behavior during the October 1987 crash and found that investors traded because of price changes rather than due to news about fundamentals.

Ignorant uninformed individual investors trading on sentiment is a common theme in the herding literature. Individuals' herding is seen as irrational but systematic response to fads or sentiments. On the other hand, institutional investors engage in herding as a result of agency problems, security characteristics, fads or the manner in which information is impounded in the market. Shiller (1984) and Delong et al. (1990) for example, showed that the influences of fad and fashion are likely to impact the investment decisions of individual investors. Similarly, Shleifer and Summers (1990) suggested that individual investors might herd if they follow the same signals (brokerage house recommendations, popular market leader or forecasters) or place greater importance on recent news (over-react). Lakonishok, Shleifer and Vishny (1994) argued that individual investors engage in irrational positive feedback trading because they extrapolate past growth rates. Earlier Shefrin and Statman (1985) had argued that individual investors tend to negative feedback trade by selling past winners.

Nofsinger and Sias (1999) tried to evaluate the comparative importance of herding by institutional and individual investors for securities listed on the NYSE. They reported a strong positive relation between annual changes in institutional ownership and returns. The change in institutional ownership is strongly related to the degree of return momentum. An interesting observation of the study was that institutional positive feedback trading is more in smaller firms.

People in good moods make more optimistic choices and judgments. Saunders (1993) showed that the NYSE tends to be negative during cloudy days. Hirshleifer and Shumway (2001) analyzed data for twenty six countries from 1982-1997 and found stock markets returns to be positively correlated with sunshine in almost all of the countries studied, suggesting that pleasant weather positively influences investor decisions.

In his editorial commentary for the Journal of Psychology and Financial Markets (2002), Shefrin discussed the results of his study on professional investors regarding their judgment about one year returns expectations and perceived risk. He found that respondents expected riskier stocks to produce lower returns than safer stocks. This he reasoned was because investors relied on the behavioral heuristic of 'representativeness'. He found that investors were guided by the thumb rule that "stocks of good companies are representative of good stocks". To verify this heuristic Shefrin used value as a long-term investment (VLIT) as a proxy for the quality of company's stock and quality of management as a proxy for the quality of the company. He found the correlation coefficient between these two variables to be as high as 90% confirming the working of representativeness heuristic. He further found the correlation coefficient between quality of management and financial soundness to be 85% and that between financial soundness and perceived risk to be -85%. It seems, therefore, that investors appeared to identify good stocks with companies that are financially sound. Representativeness leads investors to associate high expected returns to the stocks of companies that are well run, and low risk to companies that are financially sound. Because investors judge well run companies to be financially sound, representativeness leads them to expect higher returns from safe stocks.

To examine this negative relationship between return and risk, Shefrin compared cross-section of expected returns with that of realized returns. In the testing of CAPM, realized returns and book-to-market equity are used as proxy for expected returns and true risk. In his survey he found book-to-market to be positively related to realized returns but negatively related to expected returns. Similarly, size was found to be negatively related to realized returns, but positively related to expected returns. Perceived risk was found to be positively correlated with book-to-market equity and beta and negatively correlated with size. These results led to the conclusion that investors form erroneous judgments about future returns, and they therefore, wrongly perceive risk and expected returns to be negatively related.

4.4.2 Capital Asset Pricing Model

Much of the attraction for CAPM in financial research has been due to its simple and elegant structure. Central to the testing of CAPM is the establishment of a mean-variance efficient frontier. Shefrin & Statman (2000) developed a behavioral portfolio theory (BPT) where investors choose portfolio by considering expected wealth, desire for security and potential, aspiration levels and probabilities of achieving aspiration levels. The efficient frontier associated with BPT in general does not coincide with M-V efficient frontier. The optimal portfolios of BPT investors are different from those of CAPM investors. The latter hold a combination of the market portfolio and the risk free security. In contrast the optional portfolios of BPT investors resemble combinations of bonds and lottery tickets.

Many researchers have used the multifactor asset framework to give behavioral interpretation to stock market behavior. These researchers used characteristics such as size, book-to-market equity and past-returns to explain differences in expected returns across securities. Whereas, the proponents of market efficiency argued that these characteristics proxy for unobserved risk, those of behavioral finance argued that these characteristics proxy for investors' pricing errors.

Daniel and Titman (1997) used size and book-to-market value as reflective of mispricing to characterize cross-sectional variation in expected returns. They reported that although high book-to-market stocks do covary strongly with other high book-to-market stocks, the covariances do not result from there being particular risks associated with distress, but rather reflect the fact that high book-to-market firms tend to have similar properties, e.g. they might be in related line of business, in the same industries or from the same region. They found that while high book-to-market stocks do indeed covary with one another, their covariances were equally strong before the firms became distressed. Controlling for firm characteristics they do not find any positive relationship between expected returns and loadings on the market, HML or SMB factors- where SMB is the return on the mimicking portfolio for the common size factor in stock returns and HML, the return on the mimicking portfolio for the common book-to-market equity factor in returns.

The study tests three models to examine the significance of "distress" factor vis-à-vis firm characteristics as a determinant of the expected return. A set of nine portfolios were formed based on the interaction of three book-to-market categories and three size categories. The stocks on each of these nine portfolios were then placed into five value weighted categories based on the ex-ante estimate of the three factor loadings of market, SMB and HML factors obtained by running the regression

$$R_i - R_f = a_i + b_i(R_M - R_f) + S_i SMB + h_i HML + \varepsilon_i \quad \cdots\cdots 4.1$$

where R_i = mean return on portfolio i

R_M, SMB and HML are the return of market, SMB and HML portfolios and R_f is the return on a risk-less asset.

The resulting sets of portfolio consisted of stocks with approximately the same size and book-to-market ratios but with different factor loadings. These portfolios allowed the authors to examine the extent to which average returns are generated by the factor loadings rather than the characteristics.

For the constructed portfolios equation (4.1) was again estimated for the sample period. Models (1) and (2) predict that the a's should be zero, whereas model 3 predicts that the a's of the low factor loading portfolio should be positive and that those of the high factor loading portfolio should be negative. To test whether the a's associated with the high and low factor loadings were significantly different from each other the authors constructed 'characteristic-balanced' portfolios. This was done by going long on the lowest two factor loading portfolios and taking a short position in the top two factor loading portfolios in each size book-to-market category. In all nine zero cost portfolios were constructed which were then combined to form one zero cost-characteristic balanced portfolio. For the characteristic-balanced portfolio the intercept had to be positive to validate model 3.

Further, while model 1 and 2 predict that the average returns would be different from zero, model 3 i.e. the characteristic-based model predicts that the average return from zero cost characteristic balanced portfolios would be indistinguishable from zero.

The estimation results from the set of portfolios sorted by loadings on the book-to-market factor HML showed that all but one of the a's from the time series regression of the 9 individual characteristic-balanced portfolio returns on the factor returns were positive and 3 of the 9 had 't' statistics above 2. Furthermore, the intercept for the regression of the returns of the combined characteristic balanced portfolio on SMB, HML and the market was large (0.354% per month) and was statistically different from zero. The mean return of the combined characteristic balanced portfolio was found to be -0.116% per month with a t value of -0.60. These results were consistent with the characteristic based pricing model and were inconsistent with the factor pricing models (models 1 and 2).

That the market rewards adopting a strategy 'contrarian' to the 'naïve' strategies followed by other investors has been discussed by Lakonishok et al. (1994). The authors tried to show that value strategies yield higher returns because these exploit the sub-optimal behavior of the typical investor and not (as argued by Fama and French) because these strategies are fundamentally riskier. Naïve strategies might range from extrapolating past earnings growth too far into the future, to assuming a trend in stock prices, to over-reacting to good or bad news, or to simply equating a good investment with a well run company irrespective of price. Naive investors buy glamour stocks and sell value stocks. Contrarian investors bet against such naïve investors. Because contrarian strategists over-invest in the stocks that are underpriced (value stocks) and under-invest in stocks that are overpriced, they outperform the market.

Using the ratios of book-to-market equity (BE/ME), cash flow to price (C/P), earnings to price (EPS/P) and pre-formation 5-year average growth rate of sales (GS), stocks are ranked with one end being glamour and the other value stocks. Raw and size adjusted returns for the various stocks show better performance of value stocks over growth stocks.

Again stocks were divided into 3 groups based on two variables. The sorts are (BE/ME, C/P), (BE/ME, EPS/P), (BE/ME, GS), (C/P, GS), (EPS/P, GS). Once again value stocks were shown to outperform glamour stocks. Univariate and multiple regressions were run to test for the significance of various ratios. A comparison of the two strategies over a long period inclusive of booms and recessions in the economy showed that value strategy performed somewhat better than the glamour strategy in all states and significantly better in some states.

The authors argued that not just naïve investors but even institutional investors are prone to expectational errors. Glamour stocks are the ones which have done well in the past and are unlikely to become financially distressed in the near future as opposed to value stocks which have had a poor record in the past and are more likely to run into financial problems. Investors might, therefore, prefer glamour stocks because they appear to be 'prudent' investments and hence are easy to justify to sponsors.

Thus, since value stocks outperform growth stocks in terms of returns and are no more risky, investors investing in value stocks are suitably rewarded by the market.

4.4.3 Efficient Market Hypothesis (EMH)

Financial economists have debated EMH for decades. The EMH in its weak, semi-strong and strong forms argues that the current stock price reflects all past prices, all publicly available information, and all (public and private) information, respectively, and is therefore not possible for an investor to consistently beat the market.

Studies on market efficiency have reported mixed results. Roll (1988) argued that most price movements for individual stocks cannot be traced to public announcements. In their analyses of the aggregate stock market Cutler, Poterba and Summers (1989) reached similar conclusions. They reported that there is little, if any, correlation between the greatest aggregate market movement and public release of important information. Lee, Shleifer and Thaler (1991) in a study of closed end mutual funds found the marker price of the fund to diverge from their NAV. They found closed end funds to typically trade at substantial discounts relative to NAV and occasionally at substantial premia. The discounts on these closed end funds were found to be correlated with one another reflecting individual investors' sentiment. The discounts were found to shrink in months when shares of small companies did well and in months when there was lot of IPO activity.

Many studies have shown that the presence of irrational traders makes the market price deviate from fundamental values. Cooper et al (2001) showed that a mere change in name leads to a change in the market valuation of the firm. The authors showed that corporate name change to internet-related dotcom name bring about a large and permanent value increase to the firm irrespective of its degree of involvement with the internet.

A large number of studies have addressed the anomalies to EMH. Neal and Wheatley (1998) examined the forecast power of three popular measures of individual investor sentiment: the level of discounts on closed end funds, the ratio of odd-lot sales to purchases and net mutual fund redemptions. Using univariate tests they showed that closed end fund discounts and mutual fund redemptions can forecast the size premium, i.e. the difference in returns between small and large firms. The ratio of odd-lot sales to purchases also had forecast power but only in the first half of the sample period. The multivariate tests that condition on the small firm price variable showed that the net redemptions had additional forecast power while discounts did not. Further, the predictive power of the net redemption appeared especially strong for the January size premium. The odd-lot ratio had an additional forecast power but the size of estimated coefficients were counter intuitive.

Overreaction in long-term returns

In the long run, returns to stocks can exhibit either mean reverting behavior or continued growth. In the case of the former, the long-term returns become predictable. Such mean reversals are treated as an outcome of over-reaction of the market to the event. This phenomenon is usually interpreted as evidence of irrational bubbles-market inefficiency with a predictable component in stock price movements. On the other hand momentum effects in returns are explained with the behavioral alternative of under-reaction in the literature.

Empirical tests of mean reversion involve running the following regression:

$$P_{t+1} - P_t = \alpha + \lambda(P_{t+1}^* - P_t) + \varepsilon_{t+1} \quad\ldots\ldots\ldots\ldots\ldots(4.2),$$

where P_{t+1} represents the log of the stock index price that includes dividends at the end of the year t+1 so that ($P_{t+1} - P_t$) equals the continuously compounded return an investor realizes in period t+1, P* indicates the log of fundamental value of stock price index and ε_{t+1} is a stationary shock term with an unconditional mean of zero. The parameter λ measures the speed of reversion. If $0 < \lambda < 1$, deviations of the log price from the fundamental or trend value are reversed over time. The null hypothesis of $\lambda = 0$ represents no mean reversion in which the log price follows an integrated process so that there is no correction in the subsequent periods.

One of the first papers on long-term return anomalies was that published by De'Bondt and Thaler (1985). They found that when stocks are ranked on three to five year past returns, past winners tend to be future losers and vice versa. They attributed these long-term reversals to investor overreaction. In forming expectations, investors give too much weight to the past performance of firms and too little to the fact that performance tends to mean revert. Poterba and Summers (1988) and Fama and French (1988) reported mean reversion in the USA with their findings on negative serial correlation in long horizon returns.

Market inefficiency indicated by mean reverting behavior of stock returns was also reported by Jegadeesh (1990) and Lehman (1990). Atkins and Dyle (1990), investigating a random selection of NYSE stocks that experienced large 'one day' price movements between January 1975 and December 1984, found that stocks that exhibited a large price decline, subsequently earned significant abnormal returns and stocks that exhibited a large price increase, subsequently earned negative abnormal returns. Brown et al. (1988) covering a period of 23 years from 1962 to 1985 found that large price innovations, whether positive or negative, were followed by significant positive returns. In a later study in 1993 they showed that after large price innovations abnormal post event return can be explained to a considerable extent by a volatility change associated with the event.

Jegadeesh and Titman (1993) studied how market reacts to announcement of success or lack thereof by business firms. They found that stocks that did well in the six months prior to the period of study continued to do so for the next eight months as well. These winners reported good earnings relative to market expectations. The persistence of good performance reflected the failure of the market to recognize that good quarterly reports foretold of a few more good ones to follow. So each time a good report came out it caught the market by surprise and the winning streak continued. Similarly, stocks performing worse than market expectations reflected that again the market did not discount the possibility of a sequence of bad reports in the price. A rational efficient market would be aware of this tendency. It would anticipate the good and bad reports in advance and would not have to react upon their arrival.

However, after the 14-month period the stocks previously classified as losers started showing superior returns at the earnings announcements dates, consistently month after month. Jegadeesh and Titman reasoned that the market considers strings of good/bad reports over the past months as precursors of many more to follow. These, however, do not occur. After the 14-month period the market shows pleasant surprise at the unexpectedly good reports of the past losers and unpleasant surprise at the performance of the past winners. The study therefore, concluded that firms quickly revert to the mean in terms of their relative profitability and the relative growth rates they report in the earnings per share. In the short run, stocks that do well have a tendency to continue to do so and stocks that do badly sink even further. Jegadeesh and Titman attributed this effect to the fact that investors under-react to the release of firm-specific information, a cognitive bias.

Lakonishok et al. (1994) also reported mean reversal. They argued that ratios involving stock prices proxy for past performance. Firms with higher ratios of earnings to price (E/P) cash flow to price (C/P) and book-to-market equity (BE/ME) tend to have poor past earnings growth and firms with low E/P, C/P and BE/ME tend to have strong past earnings growth. Because the market overreacts to past growth, it is surprised when earnings growth mean reverts. As a result high E/P, C/P and BE/ME stocks (poor past performers) have high future returns; and low E/P, C/P and BE/ME (strong past performers) have low future returns.

Underreactions in long-term returns

The intermediate horizon inertia in returns is a manifestation of market underreaction. Chan et al. (1996) showed that intermediate horizon return continuation can be partially explained by underreaction to earnings news but that price momentum is not subsumed by earnings momentum. Conrad and Kaul (1998) suggested that the momentum effect might be due to cross-sectional variations in the mean returns of individual securities. Moskowitz and Grinblatt (1999) showed that a significant component of firm specific momentum is due to industry momentum. However, the evidence by Grundy and Martin (1998) suggested that momentum effects are not explained by time varying factor exposures, cross-sectional differences in expected returns or industry effects.

Studies focusing on long term post-event abnormal returns that suggest underreaction are also frequently reported in the literature. Cusatis et al. (1993) reported positive post event abnormal returns for divesting firms and the firms they divested from. They interpreted the result as the market's underreaction to an increase in probability that after a spin off both the parent and the spin off are likely to become merger targets and the recipients of premiums. Ikenberry et al (1996) and Desai and Jain (1997) found long-term positive abnormal returns in stocks of firms undergoing split. They attributed the post-split returns to market underreaction to the positive information signaled by a split.

A popular method of sending positive signals to the market by firms is through repurchases of shares. Studies by Lakonishok and Vermaelon (1990) and Ikenberry et al. (1995) showed that the market underreacts to such positive signals resulting in positive long-term post event abnormal returns. Market underreaction is also reported by Michaely et al. (1995) with dividend announcement as the source of information. Return continuation was also reported by Hudson et al. (2001). In their study on UK data they showed that over a long period of time it is possible to estimate, to some extent, the expected returns and the variance of returns on a given day from the return on the previous day. The post-price innovation abnormal returns net of transaction costs, however, may not be significant. The study showed that there is a significant market response to relatively small price innovations, i.e. for small positive (negative) price innovations, the next day average return is greater (smaller) than the mean daily index return. However, for large price innovations there is only weak evidence that the next day excess of average return over mean daily index return moves in the same direction as price innovation. The study also reported that the variance of the next day return increases with the absolute increase in the size of the price innovation. However, no simple relationship between risk and return on the day after price innovations of a given size was found.

Since the response of the market in terms of overreaction and underreaction has implications for returns behavior, it becomes necessary to model such behavior. Barberis, Shleifer and Vishny (BSV 1998) and Daniel, Hirshleifer and Subrahmanyam (DHS 1998) developed two behavior models to explain how the judgment biases of investors can produce overreaction to some events and underreaction to others. The BSV model is based on the tendency of investors to give too much weight to recent patterns in the data and too little to the characteristics of the data generating population. Thus, the 'conservatism bias' of the representative investor causes him to update his priors insufficiently when he observes new public information about a firm. This leads to an initial market underreaction. However, due to the 'representativeness bias', when an investor receives a long sequence of good (or bad) news, he tends to become too optimistic (or pessimistic) about the future profitability of the firm. As a result, firms experiencing prolonged periods of increasing earnings tend to become overvalued, and those experiencing long periods of declining earnings tend to become undervalued. The prices of these stocks ultimately undergo reversals as realized earnings fail to meet expectations.

In the model of stock prices proposed by BSV earnings are random walk, but investors falsely perceive that there are two earnings regimes. In regime A, which investors assume is more likely a stock's price underreacts to a change in earnings because investors presume the change to be temporary. When this expectation is not confirmed by later earnings stock prices show a delayed response to earlier earnings. In regime B, which investors think is less likely a run of earnings changes of the same sign leads investors to perceive that the earnings exhibit a trend. They therefore, incorrectly extrapolate the trend and the stock price overreacts. Because earnings are a random walk, the overreaction is exposed by future earnings leading to reversal of long-term returns. Thus, the regime A in this model explains short-term momentum in stock returns and regime B explains long-term return reversals.

In the DHS model, investors are categorized as groups of informed and uninformed. The uninformed are not subject to judgment biases. But stock prices are determined by the informed investors and they are subject to two biases-overconfidence and biased self-attribution. Overconfidence leads them to exaggerate the precision of their private signals about a stock's value. Biased self-attribution causes them to down-weigh public signals about a stock's value especially when the public signals contradict their private signals. Daniel et al. (1998) argued that stocks that are more difficult to value tend to generate greater overconfidence among investors. Therefore, according to their model, mispricing is more severe among securities that are hard to value (i.e. growth or glamour stocks) or where feedback is slow or ambiguous (i.e. small, illiquid stocks). Overreaction to private information and underreaction to public information tend to produce short-term continuations of stock returns but long-term reversals as public information eventually overwhelms the behavioral biases.

Hong and Stein (1999) developed a model to reconcile the dynamics of intermediate-horizon underreaction and long-horizon overreaction. In their model there are two types of investors: news watchers and momentum traders. The news watchers trade only on private information about fundamentals, whereas the momentum traders trade only on past price movements. By ignoring all other information these investors exhibit bounded rationality. Under such behavioral assumptions, Hong and Stein (1999) showed that if firm specific information defuses gradually across news watchers, there will be an initial underreaction. This undereaction in turn allows momentum traders make money by trend chasing. As more and more momentum traders arrive in the market, the model shows that the initial underreaction turns into overreaction at longer horizons.

Lee and Swaminathan (2000) used trading volumes to predict intermediate horizon (3 months to 1 year), long-term horizon (1 to 5 years) cross-sectional returns for various price momentum portfolios. The paper found that past trading volume predicts both the magnitude and the persistence of future price momentum. Trading volume was found to be positively correlated with absolute return. Though all extreme winner portfolios exhibited higher trading volume, this relation was not uniform across winners and losers. An interesting finding of the study was that conditional on past returns low volume stocks do better than high volume stocks over the next twelve months. While Datar et al.

(1998) interpreted this as a premium on illiquidity, Lee and Swaminathan's study found the price momentum premium to be higher in high volume (more liquid) stocks.

The study also reported that high and low volume portfolios do not differ significantly in terms of their median stock price or firm size. The most important finding of the study pertained to predictability of timing of reversals based on past trading volume. While price momentum effect was found to be more pronounced in low volume winners and high volume losers, price reversals was detected in low volume losers and high volume winners. They however, suggested two volume based price momentum strategies – (1) early stage strategy which involves buying low volume winners and selling high volume losers, as these stock exhibit future price momentum over a longer horizon; (2) late stage momentum strategies which involves buying high volume winners and selling low volume losers, as these were the ones that showed faster price reversal.

Daniel and Titman (2004) showed that the long horizon return predictability that results in the reversal phenomenon and the book-to-market effect are unrelated to past firm performance information such as book value, earnings, cash flow, sales growth. Rather they showed that predictability is linked to the arrival of what they called 'intangible' information, which is defined as the information orthogonal to accounting based measures of past firm performance. The intangible information presumably reflected information about the firm's future cash flow. Consistent with this, Daniel and Titman found that the component of returns that was linked to intangible information forecasts future cash flow growth. However, while the past five year intangible returns were found to be positively associated with future fundamental growth, the intangible returns were strongly negatively associated with future returns.

4.5 A BEHAVIORAL STOCK PRICE MODEL

Faced with information, time and resource constraints and also a stock price series that exhibits random walk, investors find that the best forecast of the future price is in fact the current price. In a constantly changing world behavioral inertia plays the important role of imparting stability in individual's behavior. The behavioral inertia approach is a combination of inertia and caprice, i.e. random change. Inertia produces highly auto-correlated time series in which random events have lasting effects.

Time dependency in preferences has been studied by many by incorporating habit formation in utility functions. These studies argued that consumption is complementary over time (habit persistence) and consumers care about the lagged values of current consumptions. Constantinides (1988), Detemple (1989), Heaton (1989) and Sunderasan (1989) examined asset prices in the presence of habit formation. Heaton (1995) used a simulated Method of Movements approach to evaluate a representative consumer asset pricing model and reported evidence for the local substitution of consumption with habit formation occurring over longer periods of time.

By incorporating such time non-separatibility in preferences, the performance of asset pricing models has been found to improve. Constantinides (1990), for example provided solution to the equity premium puzzle of Mehra and Presscott (1985) which showed that with time separable isoelastic utility function it was not possible to generate equity returns matching the observed historical return on stocks.

Abel (1990) introduced a generalized utility function that nests three classes of utility functions: (1) time-separable utility functions, (2) catching up with the Jones' utility functions that depend on the consumer's level of consumption relative to the lagged cross-sectional average level of consumption and (3) utility functions that display habit formation. Using this utility function in a Lucas (1978) asset pricing model, equilibrium asset prices are generated which are then used to examine the equity premium puzzle.

In this study, we developed a behavioral inertia model at the stock level rather than at the portfolio level. This is owing to the fact that investors rarely hold a well diversified portfolio (see Barber and Odean 2000; Polkovinchenko 2003; Goetzmann and Kumar 2004). Investors' personal characteristics, their stock preferences and their behavioral biases jointly influence their diversification choices (Goetzmann and Kumar 2004, Kumar & Lim 2004). Huberman (2001) also reported the tendency of household investments to be primarily concentrated in their employers stocks and in general in stocks of companies registered in their country as against foreign company stocks. These phenomena provide compelling evidence that people invest in the familiar while often ignoring the principles of portfolio theory.

Further, by working directly with prices rather than stock returns one can draw unambiguous conclusions. With returns, a choice between equal weighted versus value weighted returns has different implications for the behavior of the stock markets. More importantly, by working with prices rather than returns, we avoid the crucial question of unit of time for returns. Measurement choice between average monthly abnormal returns vis-à-vis buy and hold abnormal returns has severe effect on the outcome of the study. Choice of a normal period to estimate a stock's expected return is also problematic as stocks can show return continuation in the short run and mean reversion in the long-run.

4.5.1 Limitations of the Conventional Econometrics Practices

The standard practice in empirical exercises is to choose a model from a set of models by looking at its fit on the sample data. Much of the empirical work is motivated to either highlight anomalies or to explore new econometric techniques. However, such anomalies may disappear by choosing appropriate models. For instance, Fama and French (1996) found that the long run returns reversals of De'Bondt and Thaler (1985) and the contrarian returns of Lakonishok et al. (1994) are captured by the multifactor asset pricing models. Thus, if anomalies can be shown to be generated by a rational asset pricing model, like the multifactor model then one would conclude in favor of market efficiency. This kind of model selection, therefore, has little implications for the testing of economic theory.

In general, economic models are not regarded as a theory under examination and models are suitably modified to explain the sample data set. While the specification of error distributions is crucial for drawing inferences, it is very difficult to examine the assumptions about the error distributions without further econometric testing. In case of any deviations in the error distributions from the assumed distribution, standard corrections are applied by researchers. However, it is possible that the deviation be a manifestation of some other problem. For example, the Durbin Watson statistic used to detect autocorrelation may be saying more about non-stationarity in the time series data. A mechanical correction for autocorrelation may, therefore, only worsen the problem.

Since researchers are never sure that the model adopted for empirical testing is the 'true model' in the sense of using the correct functional form or including all the relevant variables, there is always a scope for improvement. The usual test for omitted variables allows one to test restrictions on a model more general than the ones being tested, conditional on the more general model being valid. This kind of data mining would, however, change the levels of significance and inferences. The pre-screening of an econometric model changes the distributional properties of subsequent statistical analyses, yielding statistics that may have virtually unknown sampling properties. Moreover, while some misspecifications can be identified by examining the empirical behavior of the model, there is no guarantee that other specification problems will not be present, or worse, that these other problems caused a misidentification and therefore an application of an inappropriate remedy.

Thus, while specification testing is important for drawing reliable inferences, the very act of pre-testing introduces unknown distortions into conventional estimates and inferences.

To overcome the problem of drawing inferences with specification tests, it is now suggested that economic theory should include stochastic hypothesis about economic behavior and error. Here, no distribution assumptions are made about the error term, except there being identically and independently distributed. The error term therefore, have to be explicitly incorporated into economic theory. Empirical testing would then jointly apply to a full theoretical system including the more traditional types of economic theory as well as hypotheses about stochastic economic behavior and error.

4.5.2 Inertia and Caprice

In the conventional econometric testing, the theoretical system was generally an outcome of the optimization principle. However, in an uncertain world, individuals lack the necessary knowledge to optimize their objective function. Under conditions of absence of full knowledge, only direct experience contains genuine information. Individuals learn from economic experiences and form a general conclusion from knowledge of particular instances. Going by past experiences, individuals display inertia or habit persistence in their behavior. Conventional econometric methodologies also recognize the importance of the past in making current decisions and therefore, include lagged dependent variables in the R.H.S. of regression equation.

While behavioral inertia may be derived from utility maximization principles, it may be argued that inertia is better than optimal. In an uncertain world, where information is revealed through a sequence of events, the cost of collecting and analyzing information are exorbitant in terms of money, time and expertise. Agents will therefore find it more 'rational' and practical to change their decisions only slowly. This period of inaction can be quite substantial, even when fundamental economic conditions are constantly changing. Thus, agents would find greater returns with inaction rather than optimizing action.

The idea that investment decisions are made under information constraints forcing investors to adapt a piece-meal approach is not new. Behavioral models explain underreaction and overreaction of the market in terms of investor judgment biases towards some specific signals (firm level). Because information is essential to the economics of maximization, constraints to knowledge are in some sense more important than resource constraints. Since generalizations from individual instances are prone to error, rational individuals would be guided by habit persistence and reflect inertia in behavior (see T. D. Stanley 2000). David Hume believed that custom and habit based on repeated observation is the only reasonable basis of action, though it is not logically justifiable. Moreover, inertia, habit and fads are known to be self-fulfilling behaviors. Such fads can explain the recent booms in technology stocks where the explosive growth in stock prices cannot be explained by a rational valuation of fundamentals. Thus, when agents are not fully aware of all the alternatives and all of their consequences, inertia or habit is necessary for rational behavior.

A society dominated by inertia cannot grow. Social and economic advances come from 'irrational' behavior of agents. Intelligent economic agents have the option of following their free will. Such random behavior by individuals creates uncertainity and caprice, in all economic behavior and phenomena. By explicitly identifying inertia and caprice, the Behavioral Inertia Model proposes an evolutionary theory of economic phenomena. Such a theory will contain a degree of uncertainity which will be counter placed to the strictly deterministic theories of orthodox economics. In the latter, the random error term is supposed to capture uncertainity. However, as already noted, this inclusion of an error term with a specific distribution creates pretext/specification dilemma.

Caprice has evolutionary value. It provides a mechanism of behavioral variation, which promotes society's advance. Caprice also exhibits inertia or pattern in variation. The types of variations that were successful in the most recent past will tend to remain successful in the near future as well, implying positive autocorrelations among the innovations. The basic model of inertia and caprice allows for both autocorrelation and any other explanation of the selection mechanism.

4.5.3 Behavioral Inertia Model

Inertia in economic behavior is reflected in unit roots in econometric applications. Many economic dataset are non-stationary, autoregressive process, growing without limit.

Defining time series of any variable (Y_t) to be a function of inertia and caprice, we get

$$Y_t = \alpha_0 + \alpha_1 Y_{t-1} + C_t \quad\ldots\ldots\ldots\ldots\ldots(4.3)$$

Non-stationarity would be reflected in α_1 being equal to one and α_0 would be zero with C_t (Caprice) capturing the change.

The caprice in turn is modeled as

$$C_t = X_t \beta + \rho C_{t-1} + \varepsilon_t \quad\ldots\ldots\ldots\ldots\ldots(4.4)$$

Where X_t is 1 x k vector of explanatory variables, β is a k x 1 vector of regression coefficients. ρ is the auto-regression coefficient for caprice, a measure of its persistence and ε_t is the truly random irreducibly stochastic past.

The inertia in economic caprice, expressed by ρC_{t-1} in equation (4.4) is the manifestation of time dependence, while $X_t \beta$ includes explanatory factor derived from theory, random forces are captured by ε_t. The current level of caprice (a function of X_t) is attained only through a partial adjustment process i.e.

$$C_t - C_{t-1} = \Psi(C_t^* - C_{t-1})$$

where C_t^* is the desired level of caprice.

Substituting equation (4.4) in (4.3) we get

$$Y_t = \alpha_0 + \alpha_1 Y_{t-1} + X_t \beta + \rho C_{t-1} + \varepsilon_t \quad\ldots\ldots\ldots\ldots(4.5)$$

Rewriting

$$C_{t-1} = Y_{t-1} - \alpha_0 - \alpha_1 Y_{t-2}$$

and plugging it back in equation (4.5) we get

$$Y_t = \alpha_0(1-\rho) + (\alpha_1+\rho) Y_{t-1} - \rho\alpha_1 Y_{t-2} + X_t \beta + \varepsilon_t \quad\ldots\ldots\ldots\ldots(4.6)$$

or

$$Y_t = \delta_0 + \delta_1 Y_{t-1} + \delta_2 Y_{t-2} + X_t \beta + \varepsilon_t$$

where $\delta_0 = \alpha_0(1-\rho)$, $\delta_1 = (\alpha_1 + \rho)$ and $\delta_2 = (-\rho\alpha_1)$

Under the assumption of no inertial decay, $\alpha_1 = 1$ and therefore we have

$$Y_t = \alpha_0(1-\rho) + (1+\rho) Y_{t-1} - \rho Y_{t-2} + X_t \beta + \varepsilon_t$$

and differencing we get

$$Y_t - Y_{t-1} = \alpha_0(1-\rho) + \rho Y_{t-1} - \rho Y_{t-2} + X_t \beta + \varepsilon_t$$

or

$$dY_t = \alpha_0(1-\rho) + \rho d Y_{t-1} + X_t \beta + \varepsilon_t \quad\ldots\ldots\ldots\ldots\ldots(4.7)$$

Thus, the behavioral inertia model is given in terms of differences and its empirical applications involve testing for $\delta_1 + \delta_2 = 1$ or sum of AR coefficients being equal to 1.

While the inclusion of lagged dependent variables is quite common, what is different about this model is running the regression in differences of levels.

The model can be modified to allow for decay in inertia

$$Y_t = \alpha_0 Y_{t-1}^{\alpha_1} C_t$$

$$\ln Y_t = \ln\alpha_0 + \alpha_1 \ln Y_{t-1} + \ln C_t \quad\ldots\ldots\ldots\ldots\ldots(4.8)$$

If caprice also experiences the same type of exponential decay then

$$C_t = X_t^{\beta}\, C_{t-1}^{\rho}\, \varepsilon_t \text{ or}$$

$$\ln C_t = \beta \ln X_t + \rho \ln C_{t-1} + \ln \varepsilon_t \quad\ldots\ldots\ldots\ldots\ldots(4.9)$$

Rewriting $\ln C_{t-1}$ in terms of $\ln Y_{t-1}$ and $\ln Y_{t-2}$ we get

$$\ln C_{t-1} = \ln Y_{t-1} - \ln\alpha_0 - \alpha_1 \ln Y_{t-2} \quad\ldots\ldots\ldots\ldots\ldots\ldots\ldots(4.9a)$$

combining equations (4.8) , (4.9) and (4.9a) we get

$$\ln Y_t = (1-\rho)\ln\alpha_0 + (\alpha_1 + \rho)\ln Y_{t-1} - \rho\alpha_1 \ln Y_{t-2} + \beta \ln X_t + \ln \varepsilon_t$$

$$\ldots\ldots\ldots\ldots(4.10)$$

The model is again tested for the sum of AR coefficients being equal to one.
For the purpose of the present study we re-write (4.8), (4.9), (4.9a) in terms of
stock prices and the explanatory variables used in the model. For each sample
firm we model prices as

$$\ln P_t = \ln\alpha_0 + \alpha_1 \ln P_{t-1} + \ln C_t \quad\ldots\ldots\ldots\ldots(4.11)$$

$$\ln C_t = \beta \ln X_t + \rho \ln C_{t-1} + \ln \varepsilon_t \quad\ldots\ldots\ldots\ldots(4.12)$$

and further

$$\ln C_{t-1} = \ln P_{t-1} - \ln\alpha_0 - \alpha_1 \ln P_{t-2} \quad\ldots\ldots\ldots\ldots(4.13)$$

Thus, for each stock i,

$$\ln P_{it} = \ln\alpha_{0i} + \alpha_{1i}\ln P_{it-1} + \beta_i \ln X_{it} + \rho_i[\ln P_{it-1} - \ln\alpha_{0i} - \alpha_{i1}\ln P_{it-2}] + \ln \varepsilon_{it}$$

$$\ln P_{it} = \ln\alpha_{0i} + (\alpha_{1i} + \rho_i)\ln P_{it-1} + \beta_i \ln X_{it} - \rho_i \ln\alpha_{0i} - \rho_i\alpha_{1i}\ln P_{it-2} + \ln \varepsilon_{it}$$

$$\ln P_{it} = (1-\rho_i)\ln\alpha_{0i} + (\alpha_{1i} + \rho_i)\ln P_{it-1} - \rho_i\alpha_{1i}\ln P_{it-2} \quad\ldots\ldots\ldots\ldots(4.14)$$
$$+ \beta_{1i}\ln X_{1it} + \beta_{2i}\ln X_{2it} + \beta_{3i}\ln X_{3it} + \beta_{4i}\ln X_{4it} + \ln \varepsilon_{it}$$

(obtained by decomposing X_{it} into its components)

Thus, the testing of the model involves running the following regression

$$\ln P_{it} = (1 - \rho_i)\ln\alpha_{0i} + (\alpha_{1i} + \rho_i)\ln P_{it-1} - \rho_i\alpha_{1i}\ln P_{it-2}$$
$$+ \beta_{1i}\ln X_{1it} + \beta_{2i}\ln X_{2it} + \beta_{3i}\ln X_{3it} + \beta_{4i}\ln X_{4it} + v_t$$
$$\dots\dots\dots(4.15)$$

where $v_t = \ln\varepsilon_{it}$.

The presence of inertia is ascertained by testing for the

$$H0 : (\alpha_{1i} + \rho_i) - \rho_i\alpha_{1i} = 1$$

i.e. sum of AR coefficients = 1

4.5.4: Empirical Testing of the Model

In our exercise the explanatory variables included are natural log of book-to-market value (lnB/M), natural log of market value (lnMV) and natural log of beta (lnbeta). Of the 35 stocks 3 stocks namely ASM Tech, BPL and Nelco had negative BE/ME value and were therefore dropped. Many of the stocks reported negative beta values for part of the time period under consideration. Moreover, the coefficient of beta was found to be insignificant in the earlier exercise of univariate regression. However, considering the fact that for long, beta dominated the risk-return models, we saw it reasonable to continue including beta in the set of explanatory variables. To take care of the problem of finding natural log for negative betas we bifurcated the beta variable into $\ln\beta$ positive and $\ln\beta$ negative. For positive beta values natural log is estimated and is recorded as variable lnbeta positive. For such periods with positive beta, the variable lnbeta negative shows the value of zero. Similarly, for negative betas, the ln value of $|\beta|$ is estimated (i.e. excluding negative sign) and this is treated as variable $\ln\beta$ negative. Here the variable $\ln\beta$ positive has elements zero for the corresponding time period. Out of the thirty-two sample companies thirteen had two beta variables of lnbeta and lnbeta negative.

(A) Unit Root Test

Any meaningful exercise using time series data is possible only after verifying the stationarity of the series under consideration. Towards this end ADF test was conducted on the price series, natural log of the book to market value (lnBM), natural log of the market value (lnMV), natural log of beta(lnβ) and natural log of beta negative(lnβ neg)

The first step involved running a unit root test with both trend and intercept. The ADF test statistic was then compared to the critical value. If the null of unit root was accepted, then in the second step for the following regression

$$\Delta Y_i = a_0 + \gamma Y_{i-1} + \alpha \sum_{i=0}^{k} \Delta Y_{i-1} + a_2 t + \varepsilon_i \cdots\cdots\cdots(4.16)$$

the likelihood ratio test of H0 : γ= a2=0 was undertaken. The order of AR was ascertained by working at the correlogram and using the Schwarz information criterion. A failure to reject this test implies the series to be difference stationary. Therefore, in the next step unit root test was again conducted but with intercept only. Finally the degree of integration was identified by running the ADF test on the difference series and comparing the ADF statistic with the critical values. The output obtained from running the regression under the above mentioned three cases for the series under consideration is displayed in Table 4.1 to Table 4.5.

Table 4.1. Unit root test on lnP$_t$ series.

Company Name	Trend and intercept			Intercept	First Difference
	ADF Test Statistic	LR statistic	p value	ADF Test Statistic	ADF Test Statistic
ACE	-1.65260	3.01103	0.22190	-1.36177	-4.45132
AFTE	-3.30391	11.79965	0.01011	-2.16278	-3.63110
BLUESTAR	-1.29002	2.97545	0.22589	-0.49399	-3.94376
CMC	-2.22767	5.38762	0.06762	-1.70677	-5.83399
COSMO	-1.81554	5.29531	0.07082	-2.18307	-4.86096
CREST	-2.60502	6.99037	0.03034	-1.61098	-3.87510
CYBERSYS	-1.41327	2.80383	0.24613	-1.31309	-4.65562
DSQ	-2.38188	6.02015	0.04929	-0.51687	-4.46176
ESERVE	-3.55981	15.04889	0.02134	-3.05534	-4.26175
FINOLEX	-1.51209	4.62226	0.09915	-2.05328	-4.59224
HCL	-0.70040	3.50963	0.17294	-0.86471	-3.60139
HINDUJA	-3.28890	11.42558	0.03148	-3.07396	-3.94296
INFOSYS	-2.99447	10.61218	0.02434	-1.64174	-4.65933
JAIN	-1.66241	3.11550	0.21061	-1.53597	-4.47584
MASTEK	-2.01687	4.45127	0.10800	-1.24104	-4.49361
MOSER	-3.58313	14.18448	0.01774	-3.05630	-4.26908
MPHASIS	-2.14019	4.79180	0.09109	-2.10937	-4.97569
MTNL	-2.73524	7.81744	0.02007	-2.09223	-6.78012
NIIT	-1.46158	2.51490	0.28438	-1.27396	-4.66568
ORIENT	-2.71885	7.61819	0.02217	-1.60495	-4.39461
PENTAMEDIA	-1.55242	3.73631	0.15441	-1.89891	-5.10155
PENTASOFT	-2.51994	6.53922	0.03802	-0.69573	-5.02415
SATYAM	-1.88054	4.20752	0.12200	-1.88117	-4.32108
TATAELXSI	-3.19582	11.00724	0.03724	-0.31814	-4.75306
TRIGYN	-1.69345	3.30000	0.19205	-1.61317	-4.01304
VINDHYA	-3.51537	12.24155	0.02929	-0.95324	-5.23041
VISUALSOFT	-1.87475	3.84356	0.14635	-1.17511	-3.64867
VSNL	-2.00977	4.26034	0.11882	-1.15712	-4.29305
WIPRO	-2.02116	4.49261	0.10579	-1.30433	-5.17209
ZEE	-1.87954	4.59670	0.10042	-1.71294	-4.70897
ZENITH	-1.65304	3.09658	0.21261	-1.14573	-5.29169
ZENSAR	-1.85018	4.18838	0.12317	-1.55714	-4.28964

ADF Critical values for the regression with

trend and intercept, intercept (level), and intercept (first difference)

Critical Value*	Trend and intercept	Intercept	First Difference
1%	-4.1035	-3.5328	-3.5345
5%	-3.4790	-2.9062	-2.9069
10%	-3.1669	-2.5903	-2.5907

Table 4.2. Unit root test on lnBM series.

Company Name	Trend and intercept			Intercept	First Difference
	ADF Test Statistic	LR statistic	p value	ADF Test Statistic	ADF Test Statistic
ACE	-1.69359	3.35276	0.18705	-1.57227	-4.53970
AFTE	-2.46875	6.42389	0.04028	-1.56533	-4.45216
BLUESTAR	-1.69387	3.44662	0.17848	-1.70587	-4.48791
CMC	-1.89377	4.46987	0.10700	-1.92264	-4.56365
COSMO	-2.31826	5.63905	0.05963	-1.74690	-4.52998
CREST	-2.41144	6.06931	0.04809	-1.25576	-4.48453
CYBERSYS	-2.45441	6.24075	0.04414	-1.09700	-4.53345
DSQ	-2.73121	7.62910	0.02205	-0.79174	-4.70001
ESERVE	-2.35138	6.58005	0.03725	-0.84192	-4.48074
FINOLEX	-2.77535	8.07589	0.01763	-1.08523	-4.95558
HCL	-1.98408	4.34250	0.11404	-1.34830	-4.60665
HINDUJA	-2.40410	6.46972	0.03937	-2.27267	-4.51057
INFOSYS	-1.99117	4.18449	0.12341	-1.27988	-4.50575
JAIN	-1.61597	3.03424	0.21934	-1.43957	-4.49499
MASTEK	-2.52801	6.89768	0.03178	-0.90305	-4.56252
MOSER	-1.58385	2.96977	0.22653	-1.43327	-4.45668
MPHASIS	-1.39026	4.30145	0.11640	-1.65237	-4.44764
MTNL	-2.60752	6.99881	0.03022	-0.92930	-4.60236
NIIT	-1.43463	2.83058	0.24286	-1.36106	-4.67975
ORIENT	-2.46106	6.27813	0.04332	-1.48221	-4.47746
PENTAMEDIA	-1.45388	2.89420	0.23525	-1.62594	-4.43765
PENTASOFT	-2.05325	4.41817	0.10980	-1.16089	-4.49689
SATYAM	-2.23658	5.21641	0.07367	-1.25882	-4.48835
TATAELXSI	-2.11472	5.03950	0.08048	-0.64671	-4.61062
TRIGYN	-1.94517	4.22251	0.12109	-2.02192	-4.44561
VINDHYA	-2.65490	7.29549	0.02605	-1.03260	-4.78718
VISUALSOFT	-2.53894	6.98864	0.03037	-0.85833	-4.51874
VSNL	-2.32218	6.08525	0.04771	-1.60426	-4.43571
WIPRO	-2.78966	7.94784	0.01880	-0.69646	-4.80392
ZEE	-1.43791	3.22202	0.19969	-1.42894	-4.47237
ZENITH	-1.77276	3.40941	0.18183	-1.77333	-4.44255
ZENSAR	-2.73857	7.66177	0.02169	-0.86790	-4.73398

ADF Critical values for the regression with

trend and intercept, intercept (level), and intercept (first difference)

Critical Value*	Trend and intercept	Intercept	First Difference
1%	-4.1035	-3.5328	-3.5345
5%	-3.4790	-2.9062	-2.9069
10%	-3.1669	-2.5903	-2.5907

Table 4.3. Unit root test on lnMV series.

| Company Name | Trend and intercept | | | Intercept | First Difference |
	ADF Test Statistic	LR statistic	p value	ADF Test Statistic	ADF Test Statistic
ACE	-2.36305	5.78711	0.05538	-1.05200	-4.58942
AFTE	-2.44668	6.56535	0.03753	-2.39192	-4.43803
BLUESTAR	-1.78896	3.66209	0.16025	-1.82017	-4.43471
CMC	-1.93344	4.36729	0.11263	-1.90081	-4.43807
COSMO	-2.31318	5.66261	0.05894	-1.38163	-4.58803
CREST	-2.49494	6.70790	0.03495	-1.37317	-4.45677
CYBERSYS	-2.11083	4.70272	0.09524	-1.75451	-4.44177
DSQ	-2.51793	6.67853	0.03546	-0.69785	-4.60052
ESERVE	-2.12859	6.03391	0.04895	-2.42819	-4.50805
FINOLEX	-2.97142	9.08200	0.01066	-0.95382	-5.02213
HCL	-1.91776	4.07852	0.13013	-1.40748	-4.56803
HINDUJA	-2.34031	6.40378	0.04069	-2.15568	-4.56581
INFOSYS	-1.83477	3.57577	0.16731	-1.44491	-4.45680
JAIN	-1.60634	2.95557	0.22814	-1.59142	-4.48169
MASTEK	-2.52703	6.89845	0.03177	-1.10495	-4.49163
MOSER	-2.29033	5.51792	0.06336	-1.38008	-4.66497
MPHASIS	-1.63825	3.17826	0.20410	-1.25233	-4.47385
MTNL	-2.57356	6.95845	0.03083	-1.11632	-4.50294
NIIT	-1.69817	4.00601	0.13493	-1.33388	-4.44734
ORIENT	-2.50661	6.61590	0.03659	-1.34249	-4.46998
PENTAMEDIA	-1.44896	2.87831	0.23713	-1.63038	-4.43866
PENTASOFT	-2.04630	4.39523	0.11107	-1.23992	-4.47348
SATYAM	-2.37427	6.03959	0.04881	-1.72643	-4.43776
TATAELXSI	-2.04978	4.85137	0.08842	-0.67812	-4.58112
TRIGYN	-2.13890	4.78138	0.09157	-1.34824	-4.47360
VINDHYA	-2.76691	7.82651	0.01998	-0.92836	-4.77324
VISUALSOFT	-2.48565	6.84418	0.03264	-1.01998	-4.48183
VSNL	-2.34276	6.10152	0.04732	-1.56124	-4.43741
WIPRO	-2.04509	6.00026	0.04978	-1.74205	-4.43578
ZEE	-1.44698	3.15735	0.20625	-1.42122	-4.47290
ZENITH	-1.69795	3.21729	0.20016	-1.68868	-4.44177
ZENSAR	-2.56653	6.93208	0.03124	-0.81016	-4.63077

ADF Critical values for the regression with

trend and intercept, intercept (level), and intercept (first difference)

Critical Value*	Trend and intercept	Intercept	First Difference
1%	-4.1035	-3.5328	-3.5345
5%	-3.4790	-2.9062	-2.9069
10%	-3.1669	-2.5903	-2.5907

Table 4.4. Unit root test on lnBeta series.

Company Name	Trend and intercept			Intercept	First Difference
	ADF Test Statistic	LR statistic	p value	ADF Test Statistic	ADF Test Statistic
ACE	-2.11284	4.70030	0.09536	-1.67338	-4.55389
AFTE	-2.38496	6.30071	0.04284	-2.47489	-4.45580
BLUESTAR	-1.98758	4.14948	0.12559	-1.93059	-4.46930
CMC	-2.00279	4.89370	0.08657	-1.09400	-4.47875
COSMO	-2.07642	5.08610	0.07863	-1.98368	-4.44652
CREST	-1.77724	3.77483	0.15146	-0.76894	-4.55766
CYBERSYS	-2.08732	4.56002	0.10228	-2.02711	-4.43495
DSQ	-1.93612	4.00997	0.13466	-1.52708	-4.47052
ESERVE	-1.83253	5.33535	0.06941	-2.25853	-4.52630
FINOLEX	-2.27136	5.76365	0.05603	-1.60670	-4.43536
HCL	-1.92159	3.96533	0.13770	-1.01602	-4.57807
HINDUJA	-1.83675	3.62973	0.16286	-1.28300	-4.52444
INFOSYS	-1.87919	3.73295	0.15467	-1.72998	-4.47579
JAIN	-2.01351	4.42086	0.10965	-0.67929	-4.67184
MASTEK	-1.92160	4.24993	0.11944	-1.99547	-4.44256
MOSER	-1.81387	5.77913	0.05560	-1.83557	-4.44790
MPHASIS	-1.85829	4.04470	0.13234	-1.89884	-4.43766
MTNL	-2.42502	6.13622	0.04651	-1.95760	-4.45237
NIIT	-2.04686	4.56539	0.10201	-0.84458	-4.60406
ORIENT	-2.33023	5.96121	0.05076	-2.31915	-4.50024
PENTAMEDIA	-2.17161	5.49386	0.06413	-1.65162	-4.63400
PENTASOFT	-2.25219	6.01159	0.04950	-2.12984	-4.43507
SATYAM	-1.94196	3.96829	0.13750	-1.95294	-4.43946
TATAELXSI	-1.82140	3.55780	0.16882	-1.09463	-4.56911
TRIGYN	-1.94429	4.19842	0.12255	-1.15255	-4.48242
VINDHYA	-1.78388	3.92688	0.14038	-0.69949	-4.55546
VISUALSOFT	-1.74860	3.27673	0.19430	-1.72157	-4.43471
VSNL	-2.34514	6.22010	0.04460	-2.30598	-4.52773
WIPRO	-1.90340	4.41190	0.11015	-0.58659	-4.58258
ZEE	-1.65334	3.72324	0.15542	-1.15884	-4.46276
ZENITH	-1.47025	4.16833	0.12441	-1.88091	-4.82715
ZENSAR	-1.33018	3.28186	0.19380	-1.77565	-4.51317

ADF Critical values for the regression with

trend and intercept, intercept (level), and intercept (first difference)

Critical Value*	Trend and intercept	Intercept	First Difference
1%	-4.1035	-3.5328	-3.5345
5%	-3.4790	-2.9062	-2.9069
10%	-3.1669	-2.5903	-2.5907

Table 4.5. Unit root test on lnBeta negative series.

Company Name	Trend and intercept			Intercept	First Difference
	ADF Test Statistic	LR statistic	p value	ADF Test Statistic	ADF Test Statistic
BLUESTAR	-1.576960	2.942952	.229586	-1.60524	-4.4406
COSMO	-2.31972	5.79885	0.05506	-1.90693	-4.43471
ESERVE	-2.14250	4.88978	0.08674	-0.62444	-4.66881
FINOLEX	-1.98384	5.82460	0.05435	-2.36461	-4.58258
HCL	-1.90340	4.41190	0.11015	-0.58659	-4.58258
JAIN	-1.76113	3.34507	0.18777	-1.74990	-4.43471
MOSER	-1.83529	3.76599	0.15213	-1.90693	-4.43471
MPHASIS	-2.29146	5.64263	0.05953	-1.93064	-4.43479
MTNL	-1.83529	3.76599	0.15213	-1.90693	-4.43471
NIIT	-1.83529	3.76599	0.15213	-1.90693	-4.43471
TRIGYN	-1.83529	3.76599	0.15213	-1.90693	-4.43471
WIPRO	-2.00838	4.43144	0.10908	-1.56294	-4.44202
ZEE	-1.98384	5.82460	0.05435	-2.36461	-4.58258

ADF Critical values for the regression with

trend and intercept, intercept (level), and intercept (first difference)

Critical Value*	Trend and intercept	Intercept	First Difference
1%	-4.1035	-3.5328	-3.5345
5%	-3.4790	-2.9062	-2.9069
10%	-3.1669	-2.5903	-2.5907

The first column of Tables 4.1-4.5 gives the ADF statistics for the equation (4.16). The next two columns report the likelihood ratio statistic and the associated p value for a test of the nature of the trend. ADF statistic for the regression (4.16) but with the trend term deleted is given in column 4. The last column gives us the ADF test statistic for the same regression in 1st difference.

A study of Table 4.1 to Table 4.5 shows that only for the ln price series the null of Unit root with trend and intercept is not accepted at 5% for a small number of companies. These are Eserve, Moser, and Vindhya. However, the presence of Unit root is not rejected at 1% level of significance. The p values of the likelihood ratio test shows that for Afte, Crest, DSQ, Eserve, Hinduja, InfoSys, Moser, MTNL, Orient, Penasoft, TataElxsi and Vindhyas the absence of trend is accepted at 1% but not at the 5% level of significance. Similarly, the presence of Unit root with intercept alone is not accepted by lnprice series of Eserve, Hinduja and Moser at 5% level of significance.

For all other series the null hypothesis of Unit root is accepted with trend alone at 5% level of significance. The ADF values of the last column further show that the first difference of all these series is stationary. Hence the presence of cointegrating vector in the regression of lnP_t on lnBM, lnMV, lnbeta and lnBeta negative can be established.

(B) Breusch-Godfrey Serial Correlation Test

Before undertaking OLS estimation we first checked for the independence of error terms. In a regression with lagged dependent variables, the DW statistic is biased towards 2. It will therefore not detect serial correlation in errors. Hence, we conducted Breusch-Godfrey test on the residuals. This is a LM test for serial correlation. Since our regression includes 2 time period lagged dependent variable, we test for the

H0: $\rho 1 = \rho 2 = 0$ using 'χ^2' test. The values of the LM statistic and the associated 'p' values are given in Table 4.6.

Table 4.6. Breusch-Godfrey Serial Correlation Test.

Company	LM Statistic	Prob	Company	LM Statistic	Prob.
ACE	2.02398	0.363496	MPHASIS	2.7392	0.254206
AFTE	2.5602	0.278009	MTNL	0.23296	0.890049
BLUESTAR	3.28626	0.193374	NIIT	4.44429	0.108377
CMC	0.6762	0.713122	ORIENT	0.83439	0.65889
COSMO	0.9238	0.630086	PENTAMEDIA	0.71662	0.69886
CREST	3.72375	0.155381	PENTASOFT	2.52272	0.28327
CYBERSYS	3.273	0.19466	TATA ELXSI	2.8151	0.24474
DSQ	1.19743	0.549519	VINDHYA	0.83592	0.65839
ESERVE	3.31789	0.19034	VISUALSOFT	2.99735	0.22343
FINOLEX	2.9755	0.22588	VSNL	2.48095	0.28925
HCL	2.1522	0.340922	WIPRO	1.99236	0.36929
HINDUJA	0.7686	0.680927	ZEE	3.2119	0.2007
INFOSYS	0.46836	0.791218	ZENITH	0.26152	0.87743
JAIN	0.26538	0.875737	ZENSAR	1.80806	0.40494
MASTEK	2.97329	0.22613			
MOSER	3.42704	0.18023			

The Breusch-Godfrey LM statistic is computed as the product of number of observations and the uncentred R^2 from the regression of dependent variable on all the explanatory variables of the model and the lagged residuals. Under quite general conditions the LM test statistic is asymptotically distributed as $\chi^2(p)$, where p is the number of restrictions. The results on Breusch-Godfrey test shows that the null of no serial correlation is accepted with a high probability for all the sample companies.

(C) OLS Estimation of the Model

For estimating the model we ran the following regression on price series of nineteen companies which had positive beta values throughout the study period.

$$\ln P_t = \beta_0 + \beta_1 \ln P_{t-1} + \beta_2 \ln P_{t-2} + \beta_3 \ln BM + \beta_4 \ln MV + \beta_5 \ln beta$$

$$\ldots\ldots\ldots(4.17)$$

For the thirteen companies which had negative betas for part of the sample period the beta dummy of lnbeta negative was included in the above regression. Thus, the following regression was run.

$$\ln P_t = \beta_0 + \beta_1 \ln P_{t-1} + \beta_2 \ln P_{t-2} + \beta_3 \ln BM + \beta_4 \ln MV + \beta_5 \ln beta$$
$$+ \beta_6 \ln betaneg$$
$$\ldots\ldots\ldots(4.18).$$

The results of the above regression are reported in Table 7. The last column of the Table gives us the 't' values calculated for the null hypothesis of

$$\hat{\beta}_1 + \hat{\beta}_2 = 1$$

$$\text{Here } t = \frac{(\hat{\beta}_1 + \hat{\beta}_2 - 1) - (0)}{S.E(\hat{\beta}_1 + \hat{\beta}_2 - 1)}$$

Table 4.7. Regression of lnPt on lnPt-1, lnPt-2, lnBM, lnMV, lnbeta &
lnbeta negative

		C	lnPt-1	lnPt-2	lnBM	lnMV	lnBeta	lnBetaNeg
Coefficient	ACE	1.8420	0.8945	-0.0383	-0.1636	-0.1028	0.1121	0.0000
Std. Error		1.2940	0.1297	0.1416	0.0905	0.0810	0.0947	0.0000
t-Statistic		1.4230	6.8988	-0.2708	-1.8073	-1.2702	1.1836	0.0000
Prob.		0.1600	0.0000	0.7875	0.0757	0.2089	0.2412	0.0000
R-sq = 0.897341 AdjR-sq = 0.888786 DW = 2.032666 Prob(F) = 0 t = -1.663								
Coefficient	AFTE	3.0324	0.8964	-0.0345	-0.1410	-0.1182	0.2196	0.0000
Std. Error		4.1628	0.1312	0.1433	0.0823	0.1713	0.5980	0.0000
t-Statistic		0.7284	6.8352	-0.2407	-1.7135	-0.6900	0.3672	0.0000
Prob.		0.4692	0.0000	0.8106	0.0918	0.4928	0.7147	0.0000
R-sq = 0.849264 AdjR-sq = 0.836702 DW = 1.915063 Prob(F) = 0 t = -1.98								
Coefficient	BLUESTAR	-13.7697	0.8489	-0.1148	0.5275	0.7692	0.2452	0.1216
Std. Error		3.9782	0.1312	0.1224	0.1324	0.2170	0.0693	0.0373
t-Statistic		-3.4613	6.4712	-0.9377	3.9830	3.5440	3.5352	3.2578
Prob.		0.0010	0.0000	0.3522	0.0002	0.0008	0.0008	0.0019
R-sq =0.920026 AdjR-sq = 0.911893 DW = 2.032666 Prob(F) = 0 t = -3.49								

Table 4.7: Contd.

Coefficient	CMC	-0.0966	0.9879	-0.2086	0.0498	0.0676	-0.0379	0.0000
Std. Error		2.3038	0.1237	0.1321	0.0744	0.1196	0.0354	0.0000
t-Statistic		-0.0419	7.9829	-1.5792	0.6698	0.5654	-1.0714	0.0000
Prob.		0.9667	0.0000	0.1195	0.5055	0.5739	0.2883	0.0000
R-sq = 0.767065 **AdjR-sq** = 0.747653 **DW** = 1.992401 **Prob(F)** = 0 **t** = -2.35								
Coefficient	COSMO	1.6672	0.5711	0.2725	-0.1187	-0.0414	-0.1666	0.0770
Std. Error		2.0388	0.1227	0.1321	0.1476	0.1018	0.1122	0.0439
t-Statistic		0.8177	4.6535	2.0635	-0.8040	-0.4064	-1.4847	1.7568
Prob.		0.4168	0.0000	0.0435	0.4247	0.6859	0.1429	0.0841
R-sq = 0.884129 **AdjR-sq** = 0.872346 **DW** = 2.053098 **Prob(F)** = 0 **t** = -1.61								
Coefficient	CREST	10.6456	0.9274	-0.0607	-0.5491	-0.5031	0.1067	0.0000
Std. Error		3.3939	0.1264	0.1347	0.1934	0.1635	0.0868	0.0000
t-Statistic		3.1367	7.3374	-0.4510	-2.8396	-3.0761	1.2297	0.0000
Prob.		0.0026	0.0000	0.6536	0.0062	0.0032	0.2236	0.0000
R-sq = 0.910739 **AdjR-sq** = 0.903301 **DW** = 2.096961 **Prob(F)** = 0 **t** = -1.99								
Coefficient	CYBERSYS	-0.0126	0.9641	0.0101	-0.0026	-0.0038	0.1257	0.0000
Std. Error		0.6056	0.1277	0.1355	0.0988	0.0295	0.1393	0.0000
t-Statistic		-0.0209	7.5490	0.0746	-0.0266	-0.1305	0.9028	0.0000
Prob.		0.9834	0.0000	0.9408	0.9789	0.8966	0.3702	0.0000
R-sq = 0.950369 **AdjR-sq** = 0.946233 **DW** = 1.960987 **Prob(F)** = 0 **t** = -0.45								

Table 4.7: Contd.

Coefficient	DSQ	7.2462	0.8419	-0.0449	-0.3656	-0.2533	-0.9163	0.0000
Std. Error		2.8389	0.1280	0.1472	0.1305	0.1214	0.3472	0.0000
t-Statistic		2.5525	6.5755	-0.3051	-2.8022	-2.0871	-2.6390	0.0000
Prob.		0.0133	0.0000	0.7613	0.0068	0.0411	0.0106	0.0000
R-sq = 0.964638 AdjR-sq = 0.961691 DW = 2.024837 Prob(F) = 0 t = -2.14								
Coefficient	ESERVE	-24.6422	0.7094	0.1346	0.8987	1.2783	0.9219	3.6217
Std. Error		89.5153	0.1260	0.1303	3.0048	4.4734	3.0649	11.9790
t-Statistic		-0.2753	5.6297	1.0328	0.2991	0.2858	0.3008	0.3023
Prob.		0.7841	0.0000	0.3059	0.7659	0.7761	0.7646	0.7635
R-sq = 0.744673 AdjR-sq = 0.718707 DW = 2.00396 Prob(F) = 0 t = -2.00								
Coefficient	FINOLEX	-16.1226	0.5453	0.1806	0.9429	0.7748	-0.1734	-0.1731
Std. Error		11.0004	0.1225	0.1217	0.4899	0.4941	0.0817	0.0496
t-Statistic		-1.4656	4.4526	1.4832	1.9247	1.5680	-2.1235	-3.4861
Prob.		0.1481	0.0000	0.1433	0.0591	0.1222	0.0379	0.0009
R-sq = 0.918078 AdjR-sq = 0.909747 DW = 2.105351 Prob(F) = 0 t = -3.27								
Coefficient	HCL	47.1060	0.7081	0.1682	-1.9989	-2.1246	-0.0051	-0.3191
Std. Error		63.5441	0.1288	0.1264	2.6236	2.8765	0.6754	0.1115
t-Statistic		0.7413	5.4964	1.3300	-0.7619	-0.7386	-0.0076	-2.8616
Prob.		0.4614	0.0000	0.1886	0.4492	0.4631	0.9940	0.0058
R-sq = 0.941186 AdjR-sq = 0.935205 DW = 2.109003 Prob(F) = 0 t = -1.97								

Table 4.7: Contd.

Coefficient	HINDUJA	-2.3139	1.1041	-0.0711	0.3663	0.1018	-0.0037	0.0000
Std. Error		3.3113	0.1192	0.1426	0.2244	0.1525	0.0142	0.0000
t-Statistic		-0.6988	9.2590	-0.4987	1.6326	0.6672	-0.2606	0.0000
Prob.		0.4874	0.0000	0.6198	0.1078	0.5072	0.7953	0.0000
R-sq = 0.919182 AdjR-sq =0.912448 DW = 1.916596 Prob(F) = 0 t = 0.501								
Coefficient	INFOSYS	1.4784	0.7773	-0.0043	-0.1270	0.0027	0.1151	0.0000
Std. Error		0.8466	0.1296	0.1347	0.0858	0.0238	0.0895	0.0000
t-Statistic		1.7462	5.9957	-0.0322	-1.4809	0.1138	1.2857	0.0000
Prob.		0.0859	0.0000	0.9744	0.1439	0.9098	0.2035	0.0000
R-sq = 0.745948 AdjR-sq = 0.724777 DW = 1.977954 Prob(F) = 0 t = -2.46								
Coefficient	JAIN	9.0544	0.8429	-0.0659	-0.8248	-0.4300	-0.2054	0.6225
Std. Error		17.8614	0.1252	0.1217	1.1730	0.9210	0.3371	0.4103
t-Statistic		0.5069	6.7308	-0.5418	-0.7031	-0.4669	-0.6093	1.5171
Prob.		0.6141	0.0000	0.5900	0.4847	0.6423	0.5447	0.1346
R-sq = 0.888267 AdjR-sq = 0.876904 DW = 1.962494 Prob(F) = 0 t = -3.28								
Coefficient	MASTEK	2.2929	0.9542	0.0070	-0.0867	-0.1060	0.1076	0.0000
Std. Error		2.3421	0.1285	0.1367	0.1135	0.1082	0.2299	0.0000
t-Statistic		0.9790	7.4288	0.0510	-0.7638	-0.9791	0.4682	0.0000
Prob.		0.3315	0.0000	0.9595	0.4480	0.3315	0.6414	0.0000
R-sq = 0.923703 AdjR-sq = 0.917345 DW = 1.915473 Prob(F) = 0 t = -0.74								

119

Table 4.7: Contd.

Coefficient	MOSER	1.2697	0.7552	0.0491	0.0044	-0.0071	0.0154	-0.0662
Std. Error		0.9839	0.1282	0.1286	0.1335	0.0440	0.1054	0.0886
t-Statistic		1.2905	5.8909	0.3814	0.0329	-0.1605	0.1461	-0.7472
Prob.		0.2019	0.0000	0.7043	0.9738	0.8730	0.8844	0.4579
R-sq = 0.772889 AdjR-sq = 0.749793 DW = 2.057018 Prob(F) = 0 t = -2.48								
Coefficient	MPHASIS	5.8226	0.8672	-0.1516	-0.0467	-0.1757	-0.6700	0.0258
Std. Error		2.3446	0.1321	0.1284	0.0407	0.0874	0.3900	0.0206
t-Statistic		2.4834	6.5665	-1.1801	-1.1499	-2.0103	-1.7178	1.2520
Prob.		0.0159	0.0000	0.2427	0.2548	0.0490	0.0911	0.2155
R-sq = 0.822951 AdjR-sq = 0.804946 DW = 1.904903 Prob(F) = 0 t = -2.82								
Coefficient	MTNL	30.4114	0.5738	-0.0237	-0.9100	-1.1147	0.0738	0.1072
Std. Error		8.6277	0.1239	0.1223	0.2506	0.3309	0.0694	0.0684
t-Statistic		3.5248	4.6331	-0.1940	-3.6309	-3.3691	1.0624	1.5673
Prob.		0.0008	0.0000	0.8469	0.0006	0.0013	0.2924	0.1224
R-sq = 0.797689 AdjR-sq = 0.777115 DW = 2.02991 Prob(F) = 0 t = -4.29								
Coefficient	NIIT	37.7572	0.7398	-0.0706	-0.2841	-1.4403	0.1576	0.2572
Std. Error		17.3706	0.1260	0.1439	0.1369	0.6851	0.1647	0.1361
t-Statistic		2.1736	5.8692	-0.4907	-2.0754	-2.1022	0.9572	1.8900
Prob.		0.0338	0.0000	0.6255	0.0423	0.0398	0.3424	0.0637
R-sq = 0.94485 AdjR-sq = 0.939241 DW = 2.061302 Prob(F) = 0 t = -2.88								

Coefficient	ORIENT	1.5824	0.9117	-0.0911	-0.1604	-0.0478	0.1549	0.0000
Std. Error		5.0381	0.1274	0.1390	0.2847	0.2450	0.1144	0.0000
t-Statistic		0.3141	7.1576	-0.6551	-0.5635	-0.1951	1.3535	0.0000
Prob.		0.7546	0.0000	0.5149	0.5752	0.8460	0.1810	0.0000
R-sq =0.842621 AdjR-sq = 0.829506 DW = 2.041689 Prob(F) = 0 t = -2.12								
Coefficient	PENTAMEDIA	80.8495	0.8670	-0.0305	-3.8814	-3.4607	-0.3694	0.0000
Std. Error		74.0574	0.1301	0.1436	3.4967	3.2023	0.3318	0.0000
t-Statistic		1.0917	6.6667	-0.2126	-1.1100	-1.0807	-1.1131	0.0000
Prob.		0.2793	0.0000	0.8323	0.2714	0.2841	0.2701	0.0000
R-sq = 0.889507 AdjR-sq = 0.880299 DW = 1.973686 Prob(F) = 0 t = -1.81								
Coefficient	PENTASOFT	42.5597	0.9719	-0.1393	-1.9722	-1.8103	0.1548	0.0000
Std. Error		17.6679	0.1320	0.1393	0.7937	0.7539	0.0864	0.0000
t-Statistic		2.4089	7.3608	-0.9998	-2.4848	-2.4011	1.7904	0.0000
Prob.		0.0191	0.0000	0.3214	0.0158	0.0195	0.0784	0.0000
R-sq = 0.973311 AdjR-sq = 0.971087 DW = 1.9787 Prob(F) = 0 t = -2.46								
Coefficient	SATYAM	11.2988	0.8385	-0.0095	-0.2587	-0.4213	-0.2877	0.0000
Std. Error		3.0198	0.1246	0.1238	0.0820	0.1132	0.1812	0.0000
t-Statistic		3.7416	6.7269	-0.0765	-3.1557	-3.7213	-1.5879	0.0000
Prob.		0.0004	0.0000	0.9393	0.0025	0.0004	0.1176	0.0000
R-sq = 0.932581 AdjR-sq = 0.932581 DW = 2.043714 Prob(F) = 0 t = -2.79								

Table 4.7: Contd.

Coefficient	TATAELXSI	3.1207	0.7807	-0.0338	-0.2088	-0.1057	-0.4263	0.0000
Std. Error		16.5873	0.1248	0.1245	0.8106	0.8370	0.1444	0.0000
t-Statistic		0.1881	6.2572	-0.2719	-0.2576	-0.1262	-2.9523	0.0000
Prob.		0.8514	0.0000	0.7867	0.7976	0.9000	0.0045	0.0000

R-sq = 0.954265 AdjR-sq = 0.950454 DW = 2.110483 Prob(F) = 0 t = -3.30

Coefficient	TRIGYN	5.1014	0.8659	-0.0216	-0.4772	-0.2191	0.6190	-0.4417
Std. Error		1.4058	0.1226	0.1272	0.1286	0.0710	0.1904	0.1558
t-Statistic		3.6288	7.0651	-0.1695	-3.7108	-3.0853	3.2506	-2.8347
Prob.		0.0006	0.0000	0.8659	0.0005	0.0031	0.0019	0.0063

R-sq = 0.925827 AdjR-sq = 0.918284 DW = 1.862401 Prob(F) = 0 t = -2.01

Coefficient	VINDHYA	10.2134	0.7560	0.1513	-0.5290	-0.4552	-0.0021	0.0000
Std. Error		16.0776	0.1258	0.1404	0.7364	0.7422	0.0158	0.0000
t-Statistic		0.6353	6.0078	1.0776	-0.7183	-0.6133	-0.1335	0.0000
Prob.		0.5277	0.0000	0.2855	0.4754	0.5420	0.8943	0.0000

R-sq = 0.950218 AdjR-sq = 0.946069 DW = 1.998641 Prob(F) = 0 t = -1.14

Coefficient	VISUALSOFT	-0.0865	1.0204	0.0027	0.0601	0.0001	-0.0317	0.0000
Std. Error		0.2200	0.1178	0.1310	0.0379	0.0000	0.0672	0.0000
t-Statistic		-0.3931	8.6597	0.0203	1.5870	3.5622	-0.4727	0.0000
Prob.		0.6957	0.0000	0.9839	0.1178	0.0007	0.6381	0.0000

R-sq = 0.966808 AdjR-sq = 0.964042 DW = 2.098287 Prob(F) = 0 t = -1.94

Table 4.7: Contd.

Coefficient	VSNL	0.4430	0.8740	0.0380	-0.0182	0.0002	-0.0757	0.0000
Std. Error		0.2729	0.1240	0.1238	0.0452	0.0001	0.0397	0.0000
t-Statistic		1.6236	7.0269	0.3069	-0.4020	3.1263	-1.9084	0.0000
Prob.		0.1097	0.0000	0.7600	0.6891	0.0027	0.0611	0.0000
R-sq = 0.948448 AdjR-sq = 0.944152 DW = 2.055311 Prob(F) = 0 t = -2.51								
Coefficient	WIPRO	0.8487	0.7051	-0.0615	-0.3749	-0.0029	-13.0883	-0.2825
Std. Error		1.1064	0.1265	0.1186	0.0966	0.0370	3.9657	0.0665
t-Statistic		0.7671	5.5733	-0.5184	-3.8824	-0.0775	-3.3004	-4.2493
Prob.		0.4461	0.0000	0.6061	0.0003	0.9385	0.0016	0.0001
R-sq = 0.939486 AdjR-sq = 0.933332 DW = 2.176874 Prob(F) = 0 t = -4.29								
Coefficient	ZEE	178.2118	0.9230	-0.0969	-7.2948	-7.2614	0.0566	25.5415
Std. Error		83.2149	0.1304	0.1319	3.4017	3.3991	0.1358	12.9240
t-Statistic		2.1416	7.0809	-0.7345	-2.1444	-2.1362	0.4169	1.9763
Prob.		0.0364	0.0000	0.4655	0.0361	0.0368	0.6783	0.0528
R-sq = 0.876331 AdjR-sq = 0.863754 DW = 2.090802 Prob(F) = 0 t = -2.34								
Coefficient	ZENITH	-51.1420	0.8431	-0.0389	2.5478	2.6038	0.1519	0.0000
Std. Error		19.6560	0.1306	0.1297	0.9720	0.9964	0.0738	0.0000
t-Statistic		-2.6019	6.4546	-0.2996	2.6213	2.6132	2.0580	0.0000
Prob.		0.0117	0.0000	0.7655	0.0111	0.0113	0.0439	0.0000
R-sq = 0.892003 AdjR-sq = 0.883003 DW = 2.004182 Prob(F) = 0 t = -2.54								

Table 4.7: Contd.

Coefficient	ZENSAR	2.8891	0.7915	-0.0622	-0.0985	-0.0702	-0.5501	0.0000
Std. Error		4.0439	0.1268	0.1214	0.1805	0.2002	0.1680	0.0000
t-Statistic		0.7144	6.2398	-0.5124	-0.5457	-0.3508	-3.2743	0.0000
Prob.		0.4777	0.0000	0.6103	0.5873	0.7270	0.0018	0.0000
R-sq = 0.94899 AdjR-sq = 0.944739 DW = 1.821649 Prob(F) = 0 t = -3.64								

5% critical values for t (59) / t (60) are -2 and +2

1% critical values for t (59) / t (60) are -2.66 and +2.66

From the Table 4.7 we see that the one time lagged price for all the series is strongly significant and has a positive feedback effect on the current price level. Whereas the series lagged by two time periods has a low slope coefficient and is also highly insignificant. Moreover, whether P_{t-2} pushes the current price in the same direction or in the opposite direction is not clear from the mixed results obtained. Again lnBM and lnMV are individually significant only for seven companies, whereas the two beta variables, lnbeta and lnbeta negative are significantly different from zero only for five companies. But taken together, the two economic fundamental variables along with the beta dummies and the two lagged price variables do a very good job in modeling the price behavior. This can be seen from the R^2 statistic reported. In all the 32 cases the 'F' test of all the coefficients being equal to zero is rejected.

From the t statistic reported in the last column of Table 7 it is clear that the null of inertia evaluated at 1% level is not accepted in the following series- Bluestar, Finiolex, Jain, Mphasis, MTNL, NIIT, Satyam, TataElxsi, Wipro and Zensar. In the behavioral inertia approach no distributional assumptions are made about the error term except them being identically and independently distributed. Therefore, we also evaluated the model using the wald test, an asymptotic test which does not require the assumption that the error term is normally distributed.

Table 4.8. Wald test of the behavioral inertia model

	ACE	AFTE	BLUESTAR	CMC	COSMO	CREST	CYBERSYS	DSQ
χ^2	2.765638	3.937172	12.19114	5.534355	2.61965	3.971055	0.209232	4.582247
Prob	0.096308	0.04723	0.00048	0.018647	0.105548	0.046289	0.64737	0.032305

	ESERVE	FINOLEX	HCL	HINDUJA	INFOSYS	JAIN	MASTEK	MOSER
χ^2	4.009459	10.69559	3.887571	0.251322	6.0695	10.78742	0.559443	6.188097
Prob.	0.045246	0.001074	0.048645	0.616146	0.013754	0.001022	0.454485	0.012861

	MPHASIS	MTNL	NIIT	ORIENT	PENTAMEDIA	PENTASOFT	SATYAM	TATA ELXSI
χ^2	7.99686	18.47962	8.347959	4.504282	3.280081	6.073744	7.786176	10.93433
Prob.	0.004686	0.000017	0.003861	0.03381	0.070125	0.013721	0.005265	0.000944

	TRIGYN	VINDHYA	VISUALSOFT	VSNL	WIPRO	ZEE	ZENITH	ZENSAR
χ^2	4.051178	1.305545	3.78141	6.341178	18.41242	5.486939	6.467986	13.26933
Prob.	0.044141	0.253203	0.051825	0.011797	0.000018	0.019159	0.010983	0.00027

The results of wald test reported in Table 4.8 also confirms the presence of inertia in twenty two of the thirty two sample companies. In fact the null hypothesis was rejected for the same set of companies which failed the t test.

4.5.5 Forecasting:

In the debate on the superiority of rational-behavioral approach researchers in the rational paradigm argue for their approach on the grounds of testability and predictive power (e.g. Fama 1998; Contantinides 2002). However, as Brav and Heaton (2002) pointed out, that researchers working within the rational paradigm seem to have abandoned testability and prediction in favor of a scheme of ex-post rationalizations of observed price behavior. Since the rational model has enormous flexibility to generate such rationalization, it is nearly always possible for the rational school to explain seemingly anomalous results even when behavioral explanations enjoy at least equal plausibility.

The crucial difference between the two approaches of rational and behavioral school lies in the type of risk that is quantified to describe the risk-return relationships. While factor loadings are proxies of systematic risk, characteristics tend to measure total risk. As the estimated β's are measured with error and as measures of behavioral characteristics use more up to date information the latter promise to be better proxies of true unobservable betas. Moreover as suggested by Daniel and Titman (1997), characteristics could have information independent of the covariance structure of returns that helps explain expected portfolio returns.

Gebhardt and Hvid (2005) undertook a comparative evaluation of measure of betas and characteristics in explaining cross-section of expected bond returns. They, however, found the performance of β measures to be much superior to that of characteristic measures. Following Fama and French (1993) they used factor loadings with respect to default and term factors as measures of systematic risk and characteristics such as corporate bond ratings and durations as measures of default and term risk to price corporate bonds. The authors explored whether default betas and term betas are able to explain average bond returns after controlling for the effects of bond ratings and duration.

The study found the bond ratings to be significantly correlated with default betas and term betas to be significantly correlated with duration. Such correlation implies that ratings and durations contain information about the systematic term risk and default risk, respectively of a corporate bond. The study found that default betas, and to a lesser extent term betas are able to explain the cross-section of bond returns after controlling for characteristics such as duration and ratings. In contrast, ratings and durations were found to have no explanatory power after controlling for default and term betas. Thus the cross-sectional relationship between these characteristics and bond returns was an outcome of ratings and duration being proxies of systematic default and term risk. The authors further noted a significant positive relationship between yield to maturity and average bond returns even after controlling for default and term betas, suggesting that yield to maturity has information independent of betas in explaining bond returns. Results also showed that the default and term factors were able to price the average returns of β sorted portfolios better than they do the returns of yield sorted portfolios.

To understand the implications of these two approaches we undertook a comparative evaluation of the multifactor model and the behavioral model. A dynamic, in-sample forecasting of the two models viz, Fama and French model and the behavioral model are reported in Table 4.9 and 4.10.

Table 4.9 A dynamic, in-sample forecast of the Fama and French model

Portfolio Categories	R.M.S.E	MAE	MAPE	THEIL InEq.	PROPORTION		
					Bias	Variance	Cov.
LOWBEME	0.08070	0.06491	138.61230	0.27766	0.00000	0.07863	0.92137
MEDBEME	0.13756	0.10098	633.50490	0.37418	0.00000	0.16276	0.83724
HIGHBEME	0.08576	0.06707	110.68240	0.14634	0.00000	0.02444	0.97556
LOWBEMEWTD	0.13154	0.10255	120.65740	0.46656	0.00000	0.21841	0.78159
MEDBEMEWTD	0.16495	0.11283	50602.81000	0.62968	0.00000	0.45957	0.54043
HIGHBEMEWTD	0.11046	0.08307	137.85130	0.34005	0.00000	0.12813	0.87187
SLBEME	0.10169	0.07480	115.53700	0.25119	*0.00014*	0.07001	0.92985
SMBEME	0.15220	0.10872	240.65210	0.38177	0.00000	0.14987	0.85013
SHBEME	0.11182	0.08761	123.29400	0.15290	0.00000	0.02475	0.97525
BLBEME	0.09807	0.07794	604.46320	0.33056	0.00000	0.11696	0.88304
BMBEME	0.15695	0.11322	186.91980	0.46158	0.00000	0.21415	0.78585
BHBEME	0.09134	0.06904	148.67420	0.27699	0.00000	0.07710	0.92290
SLBEMEWTD	0.13326	0.10808	125.88630	0.33182	0.00000	0.11518	0.88482
SMBEMEWTD	0.25316	0.16727	883.25380	0.45227	0.00000	0.22963	0.77037
SHBEMEWTD	0.23821	0.15592	559.14610	0.40340	0.00000	0.17181	0.82819
BLBEMEWTD	0.13733	0.10479	279.61330	0.39057	0.00000	0.15631	0.84369
BMBEMEWTD	0.15976	0.10392	130.95460	0.59913	0.00000	0.39546	0.60454
BHBEMEWTD	0.11756	0.08654	176.90670	0.44515	0.00000	0.20683	0.79317
LOWEPSP	0.29493	0.16282	204.18430	0.75572	0.00000	0.77583	0.22417

MEDEPSP	0.15391	0.10773	126.53040	0.68885	0.00000	0.61302	0.38698
HIGHEPSP	0.16843	0.13695	1193.70700	0.59581	0.00000	0.60436	0.39564
LOWEPSPWTD	0.20765	0.15662	262.18720	0.54730	0.00000	0.30098	0.69902
MEDEPSPWTD	0.11629	0.08485	288.08350	0.44783	0.00000	0.20861	0.79139
HIGHEPSPWTD	0.13734	0.10125	318.04350	0.43200	0.00000	0.23298	0.76702
SLEPS	0.15483	0.12441	161.78540	0.24796	0.00000	0.07056	0.92945
SMEPS	0.15992	0.11946	198.74750	0.30957	0.00000	0.10154	0.89846
SHEPS	0.10664	0.08499	1611.16400	0.25454	0.00000	0.07737	0.92263
BLEPS	0.21845	0.16651	851.02960	0.32803	0.00000	0.10908	0.89092
BMEPS	0.11421	0.07586	114.43930	0.37947	0.00000	0.15125	0.84875
BHEPS	0.11107	0.08843	176.69860	0.37231	0.00000	0.16370	0.83630
SLEPSWTD	0.24319	0.14692	196.07230	0.57486	0.00000	0.34274	0.65726
SMEPSWTD	0.29323	0.22597	370.36140	0.27703	0.00000	0.08057	0.91943
SHEPSWTD	0.14190	0.10798	11746.85000	0.32650	0.00000	0.12720	0.87280
BLEPSWTD	0.25691	0.19671	168.74200	0.61953	0.00000	0.38451	0.61550
BMEPSWTD	0.11997	0.08722	272.36520	0.45763	0.00000	0.21629	0.78371
BHEPSWTD	0.10661	0.08357	201.83590	0.41984	0.00000	0.21876	0.78124

RMSE : Root Mean Square Error

MAE : Mean Absolute Error

MAPE : : Mean Absolute Percentage Error

Table 4.10. A dynamic, in-sample forecast of the behavioral inertia model

	R.M.S.E	MAE	MAPE	THEIL InEq.	PROPORTION		
					Bias	Variance	Cov.
ACE	0.365871	0.298879	12.076810	0.072841	0.015384	0.422430	0.562187
AFTE	0.669686	0.568675	10.351700	0.058233	0.000051	0.297431	0.702518
BLUESTAR	0.363143	0.268384	6.355607	0.041740	0.021523	0.099760	0.878717
CMC	0.312391	0.238387	4.027271	0.025801	0.001821	0.380184	0.617995
COSMO	0.420594	0.318163	7.548486	0.053670	0.149763	0.064688	0.785549
CREST	0.444922	0.354843	8.273919	0.050925	0.000000	0.337190	0.662809
CYBERSYS	0.789546	0.583187	17.258890	0.118091	0.186003	0.524786	0.289211
DSQ	0.741649	0.582573	16.755490	0.087276	0.000067	0.473263	0.526670
ESERVE	0.269248	0.207693	3.856250	0.024414	0.009403	0.603007	0.387590
FINOLEX	0.213548	0.174161	3.501098	0.021038	0.007928	0.365301	0.626772
HCL	0.573528	0.457608	8.263292	0.054045	0.190545	0.201055	0.608400
HINDUJA	2.593496	2.146370	41.784530	0.207320	0.670332	0.185396	0.144272
INFOSYS	0.399364	0.310492	3.752003	0.023913	0.009306	0.253365	0.737329
JAIN	0.819459	0.693998	16.952510	0.084641	0.000170	0.118621	0.881210
MASTEK	1.306932	1.090575	26.575910	0.137682	0.140577	0.124953	0.734470
MOSER	0.277895	0.232487	4.223986	0.024622	0.001983	0.376222	0.621796
MPHASIS	0.482659	0.365158	6.284171	0.039356	0.000798	0.175558	0.823645
MTNL	0.138613	0.110670	2.243619	0.013973	0.000500	0.109340	0.890160
NIIT	0.429600	0.331772	5.640259	0.034547	0.000332	0.054366	0.945302

ORIENT	0.585795	0.461823	10.913490	0.070138	0.000083	0.562040	0.437877
PENTAMEDIA	0.660095	0.524274	10.780920	0.062769	0.002990	0.391985	0.605025
PENTASOFT	0.424579	0.313047	9.949859	0.053656	0.003104	0.220554	0.776342
SATYAM	0.355822	0.284680	4.756940	0.029230	0.009653	0.120296	0.870051
TATA ELXSI	0.610896	0.448773	21.060570	0.082944	0.001416	0.080510	0.918074
TRIGYN	0.954716	0.729407	13.279920	0.093213	0.033436	0.646679	0.319885
VINDHYA	0.287180	0.231767	6.733216	0.037949	0.000762	0.243321	0.755917
VISUALSOFT	2.678930	2.481897	58.854880	0.285069	0.857292	0.067740	0.074968
VSNL	0.498956	0.424326	7.072514	0.044740	0.547374	0.208153	0.244473
WIPRO	0.845492	0.730511	12.358880	0.064224	0.000272	0.299022	0.700706
ZEE	0.989058	0.915344	15.381320	0.076916	0.004442	0.302077	0.693481
ZENITH	0.613684	0.555449	15.311590	0.075450	0.007066	0.483026	0.509908
ZENSAR	0.604871	0.481961	13.624820	0.073154	0.000272	0.159163	0.840565

The forecasting exercise clearly suggests the need to incorporate investors' inertia in modeling stock prices. A look at Theil's inequality and mean absolute percentage error shows that the behavioral inertia model gives a better description of price behavior of the Indian stock market.

4.6 CONCLUSION

Though the regression coefficients of our model are consistently estimated by OLS (as errors are serially uncorrelated) their small sample properties are not good. In particular, the OLS estimates are biased. This arises because of the presence of lag-dependent variables in the model which violates the fixed explanatory variable assumption. This causes biased estimates. With time series data the independence of the error term from the explanatory variables must be true not only in each time period (contemporaneously uncorrelated) but also between time periods (independence). Even when there is no contemporaneous correlation i.e. $\ln P_{t-1}$ and $\ln P_{t-2}$ are independent of ε_t (because of no serial correlation) there will still be a dependency of $\ln P_{t-1}$ on ε_{t-1} and $\ln P_{t-2}$ and ε_{t-2}.

Moreover, lnbeta and lnbetaneg used in the model are estimated variables and hence lead to errors in the variables problem. This causes biases not only in the coefficients of these variables but also in the coefficients of $\ln P_{t-1}$ and $\ln P_{t-2}$. The direction of the bias can be ascertained only after looking at the value of the coefficients of lnbeta, lnbeta negative, and the covariance between the explanatory variables. It will thus vary from equation to equation. Thus, a priori, the direction of the bias cannot be inferred.

Further when both the null and the alternative models involve lagged dependent variables the 'F' statistic does not follow the 'F' distribution in finite samples. Again, the wald test is an asymptotic test and suffers from size distortion in finite samples.

Thus the OLS estimates, though consistent and hence satisfy our requirement for the test of hypothesis, can be improved upon. The technique of bootstrap through random resampling of residuals generates the model in such a way as to take care of the above mentioned problems. The approach of recursive bootstrap estimation, which breaks the correlation between regressors and residuals of the model, thus forms our next exercise.

CHAPTER 5: BOOTSTRAP ESTIMATION

This chapter gives a theoretical perspective on the bootstrap. **Section 5.1** introduces the concept of bootstrap. **Section 5.2** outlines the technique of bootstrap estimation for a model with fixed data and independent and identically distributed (i.i.d) errors. In **Section 5.3** a comparison of bootstrap and asymptotic test is undertaken. We report studies which found inferences based on bootstrap tests to be more reliable than asymptotic tests. **Section 5.4** discusses the higher order refinements associated with bootstrap. **Section 5.5** looks at the way bootstrap tests are done using p values and confidence interval. Size distortion and the power of the test are also discussed. **Section 5.6** deals with bootstrap with non- i.i.d errors. Modified bootstrap pertaining to time dependent data and heteroskedastic data are noted. The technique of bootstrapping simultaneous models is also reported here. **Section 5.7** deals with the bootstrap approach to the estimation of behavioral inertia model. We first list the steps for the bootstrap estimation of Breusch-Godfrey serial correlation test followed by a brief analysis of the result. Next, a similar stepwise approach to the bootstrap estimation for the wald test for the presence of inertia is listed and its results examined.

5.1: INTRODUCTION

The bootstrap, a technique introduced by Efron (1979) is a resampling method used to derive the distribution of an estimator or a test statistic in cases where asymptotic distribution is difficult to calculate. The bootstrap is based on the idea that the sample is a good representation of the underlying population distribution. It amount to treating the data as if they were the population for the purpose of evaluating the distribution of interest. Under mild regularity conditions, the bootstrap yields an approximation to the distribution of an estimator or the statistic that is at least as accurate as the approximation obtained from the first order asymptotic theory.

The appeal of the bootstrap in finite samples is in fact two-fold. Not only is the bootstrap more accurate, but it also does not entail the algebraic complexity of higher order approximations. The estimators derived from the asymptotic theory though consistent (and often super-consistent) have substantial small sample biases. Further, first order asymptotic theory often gives a poor approximation to the distribution of test statistics with the sample sizes available in application. As a result, the nominal levels of tests based on asymptotic critical values can be very different from the true levels. The bootstrap on the other hand, provides improved finite sample critical values for the test statistics and confidence intervals with improved finite sample coverage probabilities.

5.2: THE TECHNIQUE OF BOOTSTRAP WITH i.i.d. ERRORS

A survey of literature shows the availability of a large variety of bootstrap sampling methods. The technique of bootstrap estimation of a model with fixed (i.e. non-random) data can be seen by considering the regression model $Y = X\beta + \varepsilon$.

Here, Y is an nx1 vector of the dependent variable, X is an n x k matrix of k regressors, and ε is an nx1 vector of independent and identically distributed errors with mean zero and unknown variance σ^2. The true distribution of ε is not known. With non-random data bootstrap estimation is done by resampling the estimated errors. The regression model is first estimated by OLS and the estimated residuals are calculated as $\hat{\varepsilon} = Y - X\hat{\beta}_{OLS}$. By drawing n times at random with replacements from $\hat{\varepsilon}$, we generate a vector of. ε^*. Plugging back this ε^* and given X and estimated $\hat{\beta}_{OLS}$, Y^* is generated. For the new regression $Y^* = X\hat{\beta} + \varepsilon^*$, β^* is estimated using X and Y^*. This process is repeated B times which gives us B β^*. Finally, the bootstrap point estimator and the bootstrap variance are calculated as

$$\hat{\beta}_{B.S} = \frac{\sum_{j=1}^{B} \beta_j^*}{B}, \hat{V}_{B.S} = \frac{\sum_{j=1}^{B} (\beta_j^* - \hat{\beta}_{B.S})^2}{B-1}$$

If the number of bootstrap B is sufficiently large to ensure that the proportion of $\hat{\varepsilon}$ in the bootstrap samples are equal to 1/n for all i, then

$$\hat{\beta}_{B.S} = E[(X'X)^{-1} X'Y^*] = \hat{\beta}_{OLS} \quad \ldots (5.1)$$

$$\hat{V}_{B.S} = Var(X'X)^{-1} X'Y^*] = \hat{\sigma}^2 (X'X)^{-1} = (\frac{n-k}{n})S^2 (X'X)^{-1} \quad \ldots (5.2)$$

where $\hat{\sigma}^2 = \dfrac{\sum \hat{\varepsilon}_i^2}{n}$ and $S^2 = \dfrac{\sum \hat{\varepsilon}_i^2}{n-k}$

The bootstrap variance estimator in (5.2) is identical to the MLE estimator with the normality assumption and is different from the classical estimator only by a scale factor. The $\hat{\beta}_{BS}$ is however equal to $\hat{\beta}_{OLS}$.

In the case where regressors are random and errors are still i.i.d. bootstrap estimation involves drawing repeated samples from the observations of y and x. For each set of y and x sampled, $\hat{\beta}^{*}$ is estimated. Again by drawing B bootstrap samples we get

$$\hat{\beta}_{B.S} = \frac{\sum_{j=1}^{B} \beta_j^{*}}{B} \quad \text{and} \quad \hat{V}_{B.S} = \frac{\sum_{j=1}^{B} (\beta_j^{*} - \hat{\beta}_{B.S})(\beta_j^{*} - \hat{\beta}_{B.S})'}{B-1}$$

5.3: THE 'BOOTSTRAP' VERSUS ASYMPTOTIC TESTS

Statistical inference in a classical framework involves either estimating p values (where the p value is defined as the probability of drawing the sample from the population being tested given the assumption that the null hypothesis is true) or constructing confidence intervals. Simulation based hypothesis testing is generally easier and more reliable than constructing simulation based confidence intervals. A key objective in the classical testing of statistical hypothesis is achieving good power while controlling the size of the tests. The first order asymptotic approximation can be very inaccurate when one is dealing with small samples. One reason is that for asymptotic theory to be valid it is necessary that the p value function does not depend on the data generating process, which is not usually the case in small samples. As a result the true and nominal probabilities that a test rejects a correct null hypothesis can be different when the p value is obtained from asymptotic distribution of the test statistic. Since the bootstrap distribution is able to mimic possible skewness of the finite sample distribution, it may account for deviations of the actual distributions from asymptotic distribution. Therefore, it can be used to approximate the finite sample distribution of various large sample tests like Wald, LR etc.

The bootstrap tests have more general application than Monte Carlo tests and asymptotic tests. While Monte Carlo tests are exact simulation tests and are done when the test statistic has a known distribution, i.e. it is pivotal, bootstrap tests, though they work in the same way, can be done even when the test statistic is not pivotal. Monte Carlo tests are generally used to choose between two estimators or two test statistics and in this method errors are assumed to have a known distribution and simulated sample of errors are obtained from that distribution.

On the other hand, the bootstrap method does not require any distributional assumptions and bootstrap errors are generated non-parametrically by resampling the estimated residuals. The essential requirement for using bootstrap tests is that the underlying test statistic should be asymptotic pivotal, i.e. as the sample size tends to infinity, any dependence of the distribution on unknown parameters or other unknown features of the data generating process must vanish. This is a much weaker condition than that the statistic be pivotal. Most of the statistic used in econometric practice are asymptotic pivotal. Under the null hypothesis these statistics have asymptotic distributions like standard normal or chi-squared that does not depend on the unknown parameters. The bootstrap provides higher order asymptotic approximation to the distribution and critical values of "smooth" asymptotically pivotal statistic.

The bootstrap may also be applied to the statistics that are not asymptotically pivotal, such as regression coefficients, but it does not provide a higher order approximation to their distributions. Bootstrap estimates of the distribution of statistics that are not asymptotically pivotal have the same accuracy as first order asymptotic approximations.

Higher-order approximation to the distribution of statistics that are not asymptotically pivotal can be obtained through the use of prepivoting or bootstrap iteration (Beran 1987, 1988), or bias correction methods (Efron 1987). Bootstrap iteration is highly computationally intensive, however, which makes it unattractive when an asymptotically pivotal statistic is available.

There has been some discussion of bootstrap testing methodology in the econometrics literature. Notable papers include Horowitz (1994) who applied the bootstrap to information matrix tests and Hall and Horowitz (1996) in which bootstrap methods are described for dynamic GMM models. These and other studies have generally found that bootstrap tests are much more reliable than asymptotic tests. If the sample size is n then the error in rejection probability (ERP) committed by an asymptotic test is in general of the order $n^{-1/2}$ for a one tailed test and of the order n^{-1} for a two-tailed test. The bootstrap does better and the error in rejection probability goes down by a factor of $n^{-1/2}$, n^{-1} or even more (see Hall 1992). Davidson and Mackinnon (1998) showed that the refinements are available not only for tests that are asymptotically chi-squared, but are quite generally available for test statistic that are asymptotically independent of the bootstrap data generating process (DGP).

It has been noted by many that hypothesis tests and confidence intervals based on asymptotic theory can be seriously misleading when the sample size is not large. For example, the 'J test' of non-tested regression models (Davidson and Mackinnon 1981) always rejects the null hypothesis too often. In extreme cases even for sample sizes as large as 50, a asymptotic J test at the 0.05 level can reject a true null hypothesis more than 80% of the time; see Davidson and Mackinnon (2002a). Some versions of the information matrix test over-reject even more severely. Davidson and Mackinnon (1992) reported a simulation in which one such test at the 0.05 level rejected a true null hypothesis an incredible 99.9% of the time when the sample size was 200.

Similarly, the finite sample level of the wald test based on asymptotic critical values have also been reported to differ greatly from the nominal level (see e.g. Gregory and Veall 1985, Lafontine and White 1986, Breusch and Schmidt 1988, Dagenais and Dufour 1991). There are also problems concerning the use of 't' statistic. The 't' statistic is a Wald statistic and is not invariant to changes in the measurement units of scale of independent variables (Spitzer 1984). Thus, the numerical value of the 't' statistic and the finite sample levels of the 't' test with asymptotic critical values vary according to the measurement units or the scale that is used. As a result the finite sample levels of the 't' test with asymptotic critical values can be far from the nominal levels.

The distortion of levels that occur when asymptotic critical values are used indicate that first order asymptotic theory does not provide a good approximation to the finite sample distribution of the wald statistic. The bootstrap provides a better approximation to the finite sample distribution, and therefore, better finite sample critical values.

To illustrate the relationship between asymptotic and bootstrap tests, Mackinnon (2002) considered a model with lagged dependent variable and performed the Durbin-Godfrey test for the first order serial correlation. The finite sample distribution of the Durbin-Godfrey statistic depends on the sample size, the matrix of regressors and the values of all the parameters.

For the regression

$$Y_t = \beta_1 + \sum_{j=2}^{4} \beta_j X_{tj} + \delta Y_{t-1} + \varepsilon_t \quad \text{... (5.3)}$$

here, $\varepsilon_t \sim N(0, \sigma^2)$

with n = 20, the X_{tj} displaying positive serial correlation all betas equal to 1 ,$\sigma = 0.1$, δ varying between -0.99 to 0.99, Mackinnon showed that the ordinary Durbin-Godfrey test either over-rejects or under-rejects the null hypothesis. The performance of the bootstrap was found to vary with δ. For example for every value of δ between -.80 and -.05, the bootstrap test always over-rejected although in the worst case it rejected just 5.11% of the time.

In general bootstrap tests perform extremely well in the context of single equation models with exogenous or predetermined regressors and errors that are i.i.d. For example, Davidson and MacKinnon (1999a) showed that the bootstrap tests of common factor restrictions and bootstrap tests for omitted variables in the tobit model both performed very well with samples of modest size. Similarly bootstrapping the J test of non-nested linear regression models largely eliminates the over-rejection in most cases (se Davidson and MacKinnon 2002a). In certain extreme cases in which the ordinary bootstrap J test over-rejects noticeably, a more sophisticated bootstrap test as proposed by Davidson and MacKinnon (2002b) greatly reduces the remaining over-rejection.

5.4: HIGHER ORDER REFINEMENTS DUE TO BOOTSTRAP

In this Section we highlight why the bootstrap provides an improved approximations to the finite sample distribution of test statistics. Let the data be a random sample of size n from a probability distribution whose cumulative distribution functions (CDF) is F. F may belong to a finite or infinite dimensional family of distribution function. Denoting

$P(X \leq x)$ as $(F(x, \theta_0)$, where, F belongs to a finite dimensional family of distribution function and θ_0 is the true population parameter, the general member of such a parametric family is given by $F(x, \theta)$. The empirical distribution function (EDF) based on the sample X $\{X_i : i = 1....n\}$ is denoted by F_n.

Let $T_n = T_n (X_1.....X_n)$ be a statistic for testing a hypothesis H_0 about the population distribution. Let $G_n(Z,F) \equiv P(T_n \leq Z)$ denote the exact finite sample CDF of T_n when the null is true. Consider a symmetrical two-tailed test of H_0. The decision rule is reject H_0 at the α level if the calculated statistic falls in the rejection region. i.e. reject H_0 if $|T_n| > Z_{n\alpha}$, where the critical value $Z_{n\alpha}$, satisfies $G_n(Z_\alpha, F) - G_n(-Z_\alpha, F) = 1-\alpha$. Usually $Z_{n\alpha}$ cannot be evaluated in applications because F is unknown, unless of course T_n is pivotal, in which case G_n does not depend on F. The 't' statistic for testing a hypothesis about the mean of a normal population is an example of a pivotal statistic as it is independent of population parameters. Similarly, the 't' statistic for testing a hypothesis about a slope coefficient in a normal linear regression model is also pivotal. Pivotal statistics are not available on most econometric applications, however, especially without making strong distributional assumptions, (e.g. the assumption that the random component of a linear regression model is normally distributed). Thus, it is usually necessary to find an approximation for $Z_{n\alpha}$.

First order asymptotic theory provides one approximation. Most test statistics used in econometrics are asymptotically pivotal. If n is sufficiently large one can approximate G_n ($\cdot$, F) by the asymptotic distribution of T_n. This does not depend on F if T_n is asymptotically pivotal. Therefore, approximate critical values for T_n can be obtained from the asymptotic distribution without having to know F.

An alternative approach would be to generate G_n ($\cdot$, F_n) and substitute it for G_n ($\cdot$, F). Here F_n is a consistent estimator of the unknown F. If F belongs to a known finite – dimensional parametric family F (x, θ) one can set F_n (x) = F(x, θ_n), where θ_n is a consistent estimator of θ. Otherwise, one can use the EDF

$$F_n(x) = \frac{\sum_{i=1}^{n} I(X_i \leq x)}{n} \qquad \cdots\cdots\cdots (5.4)$$

where I (.) is the indicator of function. With the approximation Gn ($\cdot$, Fn), the approximate α level critical value for $|T_n|$, $Z^*_{n\alpha}$ solves

$$G_n (Z^*_{n\alpha}, F_n) - G_n (- Z^*_{n\alpha}, F_n) = 1-\alpha$$

The bootstrap consists of approximating G_n ($\cdot$, F) with G_n ($\cdot$, F_n). G_n ($\cdot$, F_n) and $Z^*_{n\alpha}$ are estimated by carrying out a Monte carlo simulation in which random samples are drawn from F_n. The essential characteristic of the bootstrap, though, is the use of F_n to approximate F in G_n ($\cdot$, F), not the method that is used to evaluate G_n ($\cdot$, F_n).

Under mild regularity conditions $\text{Sup}_x|F_n(x) - F(x)|$ and $\text{Sup}_z|G_n(Z, F_n) - G_n(Z, F)|$ converge to zero in probability or almost surely. This guarantees that the bootstrap provides a good approximation to $G_n(Z, F)$ and $Z_{n\alpha}$, if n is sufficiently large. Though first order asymptotic theory also provides good approximations to these quantities if n is sufficiently large, the bootstrap provides more accurate result for asymptotically pivotal statistics. This can be seen by developing a higher order approximation to $G_n(Z, F)$. Under regularity conditions $G_n(Z, F)$ has an asymptotic expansion of the form

$$G_n(Z,F) = G(Z,F) + \frac{g_1(Z,F)}{\sqrt{n}} + \frac{g_2(Z,F)}{n} + O(1/n) \dots\dots\dots (5.5)$$

uniformly over Z where G(Z, F) is the asymptotic CDF of T_n, g_1 and g_2 are functionals of (Z, F). $g_1(Z, F)$ is an even function of Z for each F, $g_2(Z, F)$ is an odd function of Z, and $g_2(Z, F_n) \to g_2(Z, F)$ almost surely or in probability as $n \to \infty$ uniformly over Z. It follows from (5) and a symmetry of g_1 and g_2 that

$$P(|T_n| > z) = 1 - [G(Z,F) - G(-Z,F)] - \frac{2g_2(Z,F)}{n} + O(1/n) \dots\dots (5.6)$$

uniformly over Z≥0.

The bootstrap replaces F with F_n and samples F_n conditional on the original sample $\{X_i\}$. Let $T_n{}^*$ be the bootstrap estimate of T_n and P* be the probability measure induced by bootstrap sampling. Then under bootstrap sampling

$$P^*(|T^*_n| > z) = 1 - [G(Z,F_n) - G(-Z,F_n)] - \frac{2g_2(Z,F_n)}{n} + O_p(1/n) \dots\dots (5.7)$$

uniformly over Z≥0. It follows from (5.6) and (5.7) that if G is sufficiently smooth,

$$P^*(|T^*_n| > z) - P(|T_n| > z) = O\{[G(Z,F_n) - G(Z,F)] - [G(-Z,F_n) - G(-Z,F)]\}$$
$$\dots\dots\dots\dots = O[F_n(Z) - F(Z)] = O_p(1/\sqrt{n})$$

uniformly over Z≥0. Thus, in general the bootstrap makes an error of size $O_p(n^{-1/2})$ that is the same as the size of the error made by first order asymptotic approximations.

Now suppose that T_n is asymptotically pivotal, then its asymptotic distribution is independent of F and $G(Z, F_n) = G(Z, F)$ for all Z. From equations (5.6) and (5.7) we get

$$P^*\left(\left|T^*_n\right| > z\right) - P\left(\left|T_n\right| > z\right) = \frac{2[g_2(Z,F) - g_2(Z,F_n)]}{n} + O_p(1/n) = O_p(1/n) \ldots (5.8)$$

uniformly over $Z \geq 0$.

Now the bootstrap is accurate through $O_p(n^{-1})$, which is more accurate than first order asymptotic approximations. Thus, the bootstrap is more accurate than first order asymptotic theory for estimating the distribution of a smooth asymptotically pivotal statistic. Equation (5.8) implies that $P(|T_n|>Z^*_{n\alpha}) = \alpha + O(n^{-1})$. Thus with bootstrap critical value $Z^*_{n\alpha}$, the level of a symmetrical, two tailed test based on an asymptotically pivotal statistic is correct through $O(n^{-1})$. This also means that when a critical value based on first order asymptotic theory is used, the error in the level of the test is $O(n^{-1})$.

With more refined symmetry arguments it can be shown that with a bs critical value, the error in the level of a symmetrical test based on an asymptotically pivotal statistic is usually of size $O(n^{-2})$. For a one tailed test the error with bootstrap critical value is usually of size $O(n^{-1})$, and the error with the asymptotic critical value is of size $O(n^{-1/2})$.

Singh (1981) who considered a one tailed test of a hypothesis about a population mean was the first to show that the bootstrap provides a higher order asymptotic approximation to the distribution of an asymptotically pivotal statistic. Other authors reporting higher order approximations for studentized means and for more general hypotheses and test statistics include Babu and Singh (1983, 1984) Beran (1988) and Hall (1986, 1988).

5.5 BOOTSTRAP TEST

The basic idea of bootstrap testing is to draw a large number of bootstrap samples from a distribution, which obeys the null and is constructed in such a way that the bootstrap samples, as far as possible resemble the real sample. The bootstrap data generating process used to generate these samples is called bootstrap DGP. The bootstrap DGP may be purely parametric, but it often involves some sort of resampling so as to avoid making distributional assumptions. It must however, always satisfy the null hypothesis. For each simulated sample the statistic of interest is calculated. Finding out the proportion of samples for which the bootstrap statistic exceeds the actual sample statistic generates the p value for the test.

Suppose that the data generated by a DGP with the mean μ_0 and used to compute a realization T_n of the random variable T. Then for a test that rejects for large values of statistic, the p value is given as

$$p(T_n) = \Pr_{\mu_0}(T > T_n) \ldots\ldots (5.9)$$

This however cannot be computed or estimated by simulation because the $\text{DGP}_{\mu 0}$ that generated the observed data is unknown. The probability given by (5.9) can be estimated if T is an exact pivot. If T is only an asymptotic pivot, the bootstrap p value is defined by

$$p^*(T_n, \hat{\mu}) \equiv \Pr_{\hat{\mu}}(T > T_n) \ldots\ldots (5.10)$$

Where $\hat{\mu}$ is the sample DGP, determined in some suitable way from the same data as those used to compute T_n.

Let the asymptotic CDF of the asymptotic pivot T be denoted by G. At nominal level α, an asymptotic test rejects the null hypothesis if the asymptotic p value 1-$G(T_n)$ is less than α. In general, for the sample size of the observed data the rejection probability function or RPF provides a measure of true rejection probability of the asymptotic test. This function which gives the rejection probability under μ_0 of a test at nominal level α is defined as follows:

$$R(\alpha, \mu_0) \equiv \Pr_{\mu_0}(1 - G(T) < \alpha)$$

This can also be written as

$$R(\alpha, \mu_0) \equiv \Pr_{\mu_0}(T < \alpha) \ldots\ldots (5.11)$$

(Obtained by replacing 1-G(T) by T). Thus R $(\cdot, \mu_0)$ is the CDF of T under μ_0.

Alternatively, one can also use the critical values under the asymptotic distribution to estimate RPF. The critical value function (CVF), Q is defined by the equation

$$P_{\mu_0}(T < Q(\alpha, \mu_0)) = \alpha \ \ldots\ldots (5.12)$$

Q (α, μ_0) is just the quantile of T under μ_0. It follows from (5.11) and (5.12) that

$$R(Q(\alpha, \mu_0), \mu_0) = \alpha \text{ and conversely}$$

$$Q(R(\alpha, \mu_0), \mu_0) = \alpha \ \ldots\ldots (5.13)$$

i.e. for given μ_0, R and Q are inverse functions.

The bootstrap test rejects at nominal α if $T<Q(\alpha, \hat{\mu})$, that is if T is smaller than the α quantile of T under the bootstrap DGP. By acting on both sides with $R(., \hat{\mu})$, this condition can be also be expressed as $R(T,\hat{\mu}) < R(Q(\alpha,\hat{\mu}),\hat{\mu}) = \alpha$

This means that the bootstrap p value is just $R(T, \hat{\mu})$. It follows that if R actually depends $\hat{\mu}$, that is if T is not an exact pivot, the bootstrap test is not equivalent to the asymptotic test because the former depends not only on T but also on $\hat{\mu}$.

Although the bootstrap p values are often very reliable and when asymptotic and bootstrap p values differ one can safely conclude that the asymptotic p values are inaccurate, judging the bootstrap p value is tricky. To overcome this problem, Beran (1988) developed the "Double Bootstrap" (hereafter, DBS).

DBS- The DBS can be used to calculate confidence interval and p value that are more accurate than the ordinary bootstrap p values. The steps for computing p values are-

1. Obtain B_1, the first level bootstrap samples from the DGP $\hat{\mu}$, and use them to compute bootstrap statistics T^*_j, j=1....B_1 and ordinary bootstrap p value p*

2. For each first-level bootstrap sample j, compute the second level bootstrap DGP $\hat{\mu}$ and use it to compute B_2 second level bootstrap samples each of which is used to compute a test statistic T_{jl}**, $l = 1.....B_2$.

3. For first-level bootstrap sample j, compute the second level- bootstrap p value as

$$p^{**}_j = \frac{\sum_{l=1}^{B_1} I(T^{**}_{jl} \geq T^*_j)}{B_2}$$

Where I(.) is the indicator function which is equal to 1 if its arguments is true and 0 otherwise.

4. Finally compute the double bootstrap p value as

$$p^{**} = \frac{\sum_{j=1}^{B_1} I(p^{**}_j \leq p^*)}{B_1} \quad \text{....... (5.14)}$$

Thus, the DBS p value is equal to the proportion of the second level bootstrap p value that is more extreme than the first level bootstrap p value. The inequality in (5.14) is not strict because depending on the values of B_1 and B_2, there may be a substantial number of cases in which

$$p_j^{**} = p^*$$

Though the DBS does provide a theoretical improvement in performance of the bootstrap tests its computation costs are very high. For each B_1, bootstrap samples we need to compute B_2+1 test statistics. Thus, the total number of test statistics that must be computed is $1+B_1+B_1B_2$. Even if B_2 is somewhat smaller than B_1, as is recommended in the literature, for any reasonable value of B_1, an extensive amount of computation is required.

A further modification of DBS to bring down its computational cost was attempted by Davidson and MacKinnon (2002b). The DBS is costly because we need to generate B_2, second level bootstrap samples for every first level bootstrap sample. This is because the distribution of T_{ji}^{**} may not be independent of T_j^*. Realizing that the assumption of the distribution of T_{ji}^{**} being independent of T_j^* will dramatically reduce the cost of estimating bootstrap p values, Davidson and MacKinnon (2002b) proposed the Fast Double Bootstrap (FDB)

FDB: Two versions of the FDB have been proposed. In FDB_1 for each of the B bootstrap replications two different bootstrap statistics are generated. For bootstrap replication j, a bootstrap dataset which we denote by μ_j^* is just drawn from the bootstrap DGP $\hat{\mu}$. In exactly the same way as the original data were used to obtain both the realized test statistic T_n and the realized bootstrap DGP $\hat{\mu}$, the simulated data μ_j^*, are used to compute two things: a bootstrap statistic denoted by T_j^* and a second level bootstrap DGP denoted by $\hat{\mu}_j$, Next, a further simulated data set denoted μ_j^{**} is drawn using this second level bootstrap DGP and a second level bootstrap test statistic T_j^{**} is computed. The ordinary bootstrap p value is

$$p^* = \frac{\sum_{j=1}^{B} I(T_j^* \geq T_n)}{B}$$

Denote 1- p* quantile of the T_j** as Q*(1-p*) and define it as

$$p^* = \frac{\sum_{j=1}^{B} I(T_j^{**} > Q^*(1-p^*))}{B}$$

Then according to the first version (FDB$_1$), p value is

$$p^{**} = \frac{\sum_{j=1}^{B} I(T_j^{*} > Q^*(1-p^*))}{B}$$

Thus, instead of seeing how often the bootstrap test statistics are more extreme than the actual test statistic, we see how often they are more extreme than the 1-p* quantile of the Tj**.

In the second version of the FDB (FDB$_2$). p value is calculated as

$$p^{**} = 2p^* - \frac{\sum_{j=1}^{B} I(T_j^{**} > T_n)}{B}$$

FDB$_2$ has a slight computational advantage over FDB$_1$ in that it is not necessary to compute any quantiles. However it has the disadvantage that p** could possibly be negative and it cannot be more than twice as great as p*.But since it is almost costless to compute FDB$_2$, if FDB$_1$ is already being computed it is generally done so as to check on the accuracy of the later.

Thus since for the FDB test, only the second level bootstrap statistic T_j** is calculated along with each T_j*, it requires only about twice as much computation as the ordinary or single bootstrap. Although the FDB is not as widely applicable as the DBS it can be applied to a broad range of econometric tests, including the J test and other non-nested tests. The FDB can be used in cases where the usual bootstrap p value is near the level of the test.

5.5.1 Confidence Interval estimation

An alternative to simulation based estimation of p value in construction of simulation based confidence interval. The calculation of simulation based confidence interval has to be done with great caution for even if the asymptotic and bootstrap errors agree, there can be large differences in the corresponding confidence intervals if the bootstrap distribution is significantly skewed and the asymptotic distribution is normal. Moreover, there are many more ways to construct bootstrap confidence interval than there are to perform bootstrap tests. Given a procedure for generating the bootstrap data, it is very straightforward to compute a bootstrap p value or a bootstrap critical value. In contrast, there are many alternative ways to compute bootstrap confidence interval and they may yield quite different results. In general, for a given model and data set, bootstrap tests using p values are generally more reliable than the ones using bootstrap confidence intervals.

The percentile method is the simplest method for construction of confidence intervals. The $(1-2\alpha)$ confidence interval is the interval between 100α and $100(1-\alpha)$ percentiles of the bootstrap distribution of $\hat{\theta}^*$, the bootstrap estimate of θ. The unsatisfactory small sample performance of this method as reported by Diciccio and Romano (1988) led the development of bias corrected percentile method by Efron. However, this method was also not satisfactory and as Schenker (1985) showed that the coverage probabilities of the BC intervals are substantially below the nominal levels in small samples. To improve the BC intervals, Efron (1987) proposed the accelerated bias corrected percentile (BCa) method. Diciccio and Tibschirani (1987) showed that the method is a combination of a variance-stabilizing transformation and a skeweness-reducing transformation. They also presented a computationally simpler procedure (BC^0_a interval), which is asymptotically equivalent to the BC interval. Veall (1987a) was one of the first to construct confidence intervals using the percentile method. He also did a Monte-carlo study (Veall, 1987b) for his study on electricity demand and reported similar results. However, others like Eakin, McMillen and Buono (1990) found percentile method to be no different from Efron's bias controlled method. Eakin et al. concluded that rather than different bootstrap methods, it is the use of bootstrap standard deviation which influences the results.

In addition to the above percentile methods there are also "pivotal methods" which are used for constructing bootstrap confidence intervals. Of the two pivotal methods, namely, the bootstrap-t (also known as percentile-t) and Beran's B method (Beran 1987, 1988) the former is more and is widely used.

The idea behind bootstrap-t method is that instead of using the bootstrap distribution of $\hat{\theta}$, one uses the bootstrap distribution of the 'studentized' statistic

$t = \sqrt{n}\,(\hat{\theta} - \theta)/s$, where s^2 is a consistent estimate of the variance of $\sqrt{n}$ (c- θ). This method gives more reliable confidence intervals. The usual way of constructing the confidence interval for θ_0, whose sample estimate is $\hat{\theta}$ and standard error is S_θ is given by

$$[\hat{\theta} - S_\theta\, t_{\alpha/2},\ \hat{\theta} + S_\theta\, t_{\alpha/2}] \quad\text{...................} \quad (5.15)$$

where α is the level of significance.

A bootstrap t confidence interval is constructed in a similar way. The only difference is that the quantiles of the theoretical distribution are replaced by quantiles of a bootstrap distribution. The bootstrap -t is obtained by inverting t statistics with critical values that are quantiles of a distribution of bootstrap t statistics. The steps required are as follows:

1. Estimate the model without restrictions to compute $\hat{\theta}$, S_θ and whatever other quantiles are needed to generate bootstrap samples.

2. Generate B bootstrap samples and for each sample estimate the unrestricted model to obtain $\hat{\theta}_j{}^*$ and calculate the bootstrap test statistic $t_j^* = \dfrac{\hat{\theta}_j^* - \hat{\theta}}{S_j^*}$

Where $S_j{}^*$ is the standard error for each bootstrap sample

3. Find $t^*{}_{\alpha/2}$ and $t^*{}_{1-\alpha/2}$, the $\alpha/2$ and $1-\alpha/2$ quantiles of the $t_j{}^*$

4. Calculate the bootstrap t interval as

$[\hat{\theta} - S_\theta\, t^*{}_{1-\alpha/2},\ \hat{\theta} - S_\theta\, t^*{}_{\alpha/2}]$ or equivalently as

$$[\hat{\theta} - S_\theta t^*_{\alpha/2}, \hat{\theta} + S_\theta t^*_{\alpha/2}] \quad\text{.......} \quad (5.16)$$

The bootstrap-t interval is appealing because its construction is similar to the standard confidence interval constructed as given in (5.15). Further if the test statistic $t = \hat{\theta} - \theta_0/S_\theta$ is asymptotically pivotal then it can be shown that the bootstrap t interval based on it will be asymptotically valid. In fact Beran (1988) showed that by using critical values from the resulting bootstrap distribution one obtains tests whose finite sample sizes are closer to the nominal size than are tests with asymptotic critical values. Moreover, its accuracy will increase more rapidly as the sample size increases than that of the standard interval (5.15) when the latter is valid only asymptotically. In the unlikely event that the t statistic is exactly pivotal a bootstrap-t interval based on it will be exact. Also when $\hat{\theta}$ is biased, the bootstrap-t interval tends to correct the bias. Suppose $E(\hat{\theta})<\theta$ then $t^*_{\alpha/2}$ will be a larger negative number than $t_{\alpha/2}$ and $t^*_{1-\alpha/2}$ will be a smaller positive number than $t_{1-\alpha/2}$. If so, both the limits bootstrap-t interval will be larger than the corresponding limits of an asymptotic interval given by (5.15). As noted the errors based on the bootstrap critical values are of $O(n^{-1})$ whereas with asymptotic distribution, they are of $O(n^{-1/2})$. By approximately iterating the bootstrap one can obtain further improvements in accuracy. For example, Beran (1987, 1988), showed that with pre-pivoting one can obtain size errors of $O(n^{-3/2})$. Beran (1990) suggested further iteration and showed that this method called the B2 method performs better than the original B method.

However, the actual performance of bootstrap t intervals in finite samples is often not as good as the theory suggests. These intervals generally work well if the test statistic on which they are based is approximately pivotal. If this is not the case the distribution of t^*_j may differ substantially from the distribution of $t(\theta_0)$ and the bootstrap t interval may be quite inaccurate.

Another widely used bootstrap confidence-interval is the bias corrected bootstrap interval obtained by calculating the bootstrap standard error. The bootstrap standard error which is simply the standard deviation of bootstrap estimates $\hat{\theta}^*_j$ is given as

$$S^*_\theta = \sqrt{\frac{\sum_{j=1}^{B}(\hat{\theta}^*_j - \overline{\theta}^*)^2}{B-1}} \quad \text{Where } \overline{\theta}^* = \frac{\sum_{j=1}^{B}\hat{\theta}^*_j}{B} \quad \text{....... (5.17)}$$

The bias- corrected bootstrap interval is then given as

$$[2\hat{\theta} - \overline{\theta}^* - S^*_\theta t_{\alpha/2}, 2\hat{\theta} - \overline{\theta}^* + S^*_\theta t_{\alpha/2}] \quad \text{....... (5.18)}$$

The interval is similar to the standard confidence interval but it is centered on the bias corrected estimate $2\hat{\theta} - \overline{\theta}^*$ and it uses the bootstrap standard S^*_θ error instead of S_θ. The bias corrected estimate used in (5.18) is obtained by subtracting the estimated bias $\overline{\theta}^{**} - \theta^*$ from $\hat{\theta}$. In theory the interval (5.18) should generally not work as well as the bootstrap t interval (5.16) but it may actually work better when S_θ is unreliable and it can be used in situations where S_θ cannot be computed at all.

Because neither bootstrap t intervals nor intervals based on bootstrap standard error (with or without bias correction) always perform well, many other types of bootstrap confidence intervals have been proposed. However, Hall (1988) and Martin (1990) among others have shown the percentile-t method, Beran's B method and the BC_a method to be asymptotically superior to the other methods. Efron (1987) and Beran (1988) and Diciccio and Tibshirani (1987) show the small sample performance of these methods to be quite acceptable.

5.5.2 Size distortion of the test

Even when it is known theoretically that the bootstrap provides refinements of a given order, the size distortion of a bootstrap test may vary considerably according to circumstances. Size distortion means the difference between the nominal size of the test and its actual rejection probability or ERP. As noted the ERP of a bootstrap test is usually less than that of an asymptotic test. The theoretical literature on the finite sample performance of bootstrap tests such as Beran (1988) and Hall and Titterington (1989) is primarily concerned with the rate at which ERP of bootstrap a test declines as the sample size increases. It has been shown that in a variety of circumstances the ERP of bootstrap tests declines more rapidly than the ERP of the corresponding asymptotic test.

Suppose the test statistic of interest T has a finite sample distribution which depends on just one unknown parameter, say θ. The shape of the RPF (which is the graph of rejection probability of asymptotic test as a function of θ) indicates the performance of the bootstrap test. A flat RPF implies that the T is pivotal, and that the bootstrap test will work perfectly. On the other hand if the RPF is not flat, then the bootstrap test will not work perfectly because the distribution of T^* (bootstrap estimate of T) which is based on estimate of $\hat{\theta}$ will differ from the distribution of T, which is based on the unknown true value θ_0.

Davidson and MacKinnon (1999b) showed that as the sample size increases the ERP of a bootstrap test improved more rapidly than that of an asymptotic test based on the same test statistic. This is because the ERP of a bootstrap test depends on the slope of the RPF, but only if $\hat{\theta}$ is biased and on its curvature, whether or not $\hat{\theta}$ is biased. Whenever T is asymptotically pivotal the RPF must converge to a horizontal line as the sample size tends to infinity. The fact that the slope and curvature of RPF becomes smaller as the sample size increases would, by itself cause the ERP of the bootstrap test to decrease at the same rate as the ERP of the asymptotic test. But increasing the sample size also causes both the bias and the variance of $\hat{\theta}$ to decrease. This further reduces the ERP of a bootstrap test, but it has no effect on the ERP of the asymptotic test.

This, however, does not mean that a bootstrap test will always outperform the corresponding asymptotic test. There may well be values of θ for which the latter scores over the former. However, if the ERP of the asymptotic test is large, then it is increasingly likely as the sample size increases that the ERP of a bootstrap test based on it will be smaller.

5.5.3 Power of the bootstrap test

One important criteria used to evaluate the performance of a test is its power. The probability that a test will reject the null hypothesis when some alternative is true is called its power. Bootstrapping a test will reduce its power, whenever B, the number of bootstrap sample is finite. More importantly if an asymptotic test over-rejects under the null, a bootstrap test based on it will reject less often both under the null and many alternatives. Conversely, if an asymptotic test under-rejects the null a bootstrap based test will reject more often. There is no reason to believe that bootstrapping a test using a large value of B will reduce its power more substantially than will any other method of improving its finite sample properties under the null.

The relationship between the power of bootstrap and asymptotic test is studied in Davidson and MacKinnon (2005). It is shown that if the power of an asymptotic test is adjusted in a plausible way to account for its tendency to over-reject or under-reject under the null, then the resulting level-adjusted power is very similar to the power of bootstrap test based on the same underlying test statistic. Thus, if bootstrapping does result in a loss of power when B is large, that loss arises simply because bootstrapping corrects the tendency of the asymptotic test to over-reject.

The power of simulation-based test generally increases with B. However as Davidson and MacKinnon (2000) discuss, any loss of power is generally quite modest except perhaps when B is a very small number.

5.6: BOOTSTRAP METHOD WITH NON- i.i.d ERRORS

The standard bootstrap methods assume that the underlying distributions are i.i.d. Much of the econometric work is related to dependent and heterogeneous data. Further, logit, probit, tobit and several limited dependent variable model are also popularly used. In all these situations bootstrap methods need to be modified to produce reliable estimates.

5.6.1 Time dependency in data

When the error terms in the model are serially correlated, bootstrap sampling should be done in such a way that the bootstrap error terms display the same sort of serial correlation as the real ones. Considering the fact that one doesn't know how the real terms were generated, special bootstrap methods have to be used to take care of this problem.

One method calls for resampling error terms recursively to preserve the serial relationship in error terms such a method is called recursive bootstrap and is very useful if the structure of serial correlation is known and also for the model with lagged dependent variables. Veall (1986) considers the following first-order autocorrelation model

$$Y = X\beta + \varepsilon_t \quad \text{....... (5.19) and}$$

$$\varepsilon_t = \rho\varepsilon_{t-1} + v_t \quad \text{....... (5.20)}$$

Where $-1<\rho<1$ and v_t is i.i.d with mean zero. The model is first estimated by feasible 'Generalized Least Squares' (GLS) or the cochrane-orcutt transformation to compute $\hat{\beta}, \hat{\rho}, \hat{\varepsilon}$, and $\hat{v}$. Second, the independent residuals v_t are resampled with replacement, giving the bootstrap residuals v^*. Then one residual is randomly selected from v^* and divided by $(1-\rho^2)^{1/2}$ to become $\hat{\varepsilon}_1$. The ε^* are recursively computed by (5.20) and Y* is constructed by substituting $\hat{\beta}$ and ε^*in equation (5.19). Now β^* is re-estimated using Y* and X. The above mentioned steps are repeated B times and the bootstrap estimator is calculated as

$$\hat{\beta}_{b,x} = \frac{\sum \beta_i^*}{B}$$

Veall (1986) however, found that the finite sample performance of his bootstrap was no better than that of the asymptotic GLS. In a related study Rayner (1990) bootstrapped the estimated t values, $\hat{\beta}/\text{S.E.}(\hat{\beta})$, instead of the raw coefficient $\hat{\beta}$ and showed good small sample performance of the recursive bootstrap method. A further advantage of this method is its applicability to higher order autocorrelation with a known structure.

Thus by bootstrapping ' t', an asymptotically pivotal statistic, Rayner obtained a higher order approximation to the finite sample distribution of 't', whereas, Veall's results are as good as those from the asymptotic theory. Further for samples of moderate size, Veall's method will not work for higher order autocorrelation. Here the AR(p) approximation may not be a good one; and even if it is the parameter estimates are certain to be biased. Thus, it is likely that the bootstrap samples will differ from the real ones in an important respect.

A second approach, which is fully non-parametric, is to resample groups of residuals. Conceptually one of the simplest such methods is the block bootstrap, which has been proposed in various forms by Carlstein (1986), Kunsch (1989), Politis and Romano (1994) and a number of other authors.

In the Carlstein method a block of length l is chosen and the data of n observations (residuals) is divided into non-overlapping blocks each of length l. Select b of these blocks by resampling with replacements of all the blocks. This process is repeated B times and the model is reworked like the standard bootstrap. In the moving block bootstrap of Kunsch (1989) and Liu and Singh (1992), n-l+1 blocks are formed by allowing for overlapping of blocks. The blocks are then resampled with replacements to create bootstrap blocks.

Kunsch (1989) and Lahiri (1991) show the validity of moving block bootstrap in stationary univariate case. Lahiri (1992) extends the proof to the non-stationary case. Shi and Shao (1988) and Moore and Rais (1990) proposed different versions of bootstrap of m-dependence and for uniform mixing, respectively.

An alternate approach to take care of the failure of block bootstrap to replicate the dependence structure of the original is by modifying the original sample statistic. A Cowles foundation discussion paper by Andrews (2002) elaborates on this idea by introducing block statistics that possess the same features as the block bootstrap versions of these statistics. This application of block bootstrap to block statistic is referred to as block-block bootstrap. The asymptotic refinements of the block-block bootstrap are shown to be greater than those obtained with block bootstrap and close to those obtained with non-parametric i.i.d bootstrap and parametric bootstrap. Independence of the bootstrap blocks mimics the asymptotic independence of the original sample blocks sufficiently well to take care of the join-point problem, i.e. independence between blocks fails to mimic the dependence in the original sample. That is join points do not affect the magnitude of the asymptotic refinements of the block-block bootstrap.

A block statistic is constructed by taking a statistic that depends on one or more sample averages and replacing the sample averages with averages with some summands deleted. Let l denote the block length to be used by the bootstrap. We take l such that $l = l_n \to \infty$ as $n \to \infty$. The join points of the block bootstrap sample are $l+1$, $2l+1$.....$(b-1)l$ where b is the number of blocks and $n=bl$. We delete the $[\prod l]$ summands before each of its join points where $[\prod l]$ denotes the smallest integer greater than or equal to $\prod l$, $\prod \in (0.1)$ and $\prod = \prod_n \to 0$ and $\prod l$-c $\log(n) \to \infty$ as $n \to \infty$ for all constants $o<c<\infty$. Here $\prod$ is the fraction of observations that are deleted from each block and from the whole sample.

Although the block-block bootstrap solves the joint-point problem, the block-block bootstrap yields moments that are more variable than moments under the non-parametric i.i.d bootstrap distribution just as the standard block bootstrap does. In consequence the asymptotic refinements obtained by the block-block bootstrap still depend of the block length. In particular they are decreasing in the block length. Suppose $l \propto n^\gamma$ for some $0<\gamma<1$, Andrews showed that the ERP of a one sided bootstrap t test using the block-block bootstrap is $O(n^{-1/2-\xi})$ for all $\xi < 1/2 - \gamma$. In consequence if γ is taken close to zero the ERP is close to $O [N^{-1}\}$, which is the ERP of a one sided non-parametric i.i.d bootstrap 't' test.

In practice one has to use a block length l and a deletion fraction $\prod$ that are large enough to accommodate the dependency in the data. Hence one cannot just take γ arbitrarily close to zero. Thus, the above asymptotic result does not imply that one would expect block-block bootstrap to work as well as the non-parametric i.i.d bootstrap does with i.i.d data. However, it does suggest that the block-block bootstrap should have smaller ERPs when $\gamma<1/4$ than does the block bootstrap and it should outperform the block bootstrap in terms of confidence interval coverage probabilities.

Similarly, bootstrap methods have to be modified for dealing with co-integration exercises. For even if a co-integrating vector is found such that errors are I[0], it does not mean that the errors are i.i.d. Thus, one must either specify the error structure or modify the bootstrap method suitably.

Basava et al. (1991a) examined the case of unit roots that is $|\alpha| = 1$ in the regression $Y_t = \alpha Y_{t-1} + \varepsilon_t$. They found that the bootstrap estimate of α does not converge to the standard wiener process, but converges to a random distribution, even if $\hat{\varepsilon}_t$ is normally distributed. They argued that bootstrap estimation is asymptotically invalid when $|\alpha| = 1$ and that one should exercise caution in applying bootstrap procedures to autoregressive models when the root is suspected to be close to 1. Ferretti and Romo (1992) proposed a bootstrap resampling scheme for this model and proved its asymptotic validity. In a subsequent paper Basava et al (1991b) suggested a sequential bootstrap procedure for the estimation of the parameter α in the explosive case. They established the asymptotic validity of this procedure for all $|\alpha| <=1$. Earlier Basava et al. (1989) analyzed the case of explosive roots i.e. $[|\alpha| >1]$. They found that the bootstrap estimator has the same asymptotic distribution as the least square estimator.

Canepa and O'Brien (2000) proposed the use of bootstrap hypothesis testing to reduce size distortions of the test for linear restrictions on the co-integrating space in an experimental design where at most two co integrating vectors are possible. In this paper the authors investigated the size distortion of the LR and W test of Johansen (1988) and Johansen and Juseleius (1990) as also the F test of Podivinksky (1992) in finite samples. Further, the robustness of the bootstrap test to misspecification in the number of co-integrating relationship is analyzed. In particular the authors evaluated the bootstrap test via Monte Carlo simulations in situations where there is a possible mismatch between the number of co integrating vectors entering the restricted model and the number of co integrating vectors entering the DGP i.e. the number of co integrating relationship is under fitted or over fitted.

The model estimated is A VAR (1) defined by

$$\Delta Y_t = \prod Y_{t-1} + \alpha + \varepsilon_t \quad \text{.......} \quad (5.21)$$

Where Y_t and Y_{t-1} are vectors, α is a vector of intercepts and $\varepsilon_t \sim$ i.i.d N (0, 1). When testing for linear restrictions on co integrating vectors the true DGP is not known. Since the null model and consequently the DGP is unknown, the estimated DGP is used. In this case the estimated error correction model is

$$\Delta Y_t = \hat{\gamma}\hat{\beta} Y_{t-1} + \hat{\alpha} + \hat{\varepsilon}_t \quad \text{.......} \quad (5.22)$$

Where $\hat{\gamma}$ and $\hat{\beta}$ are the estimates for a given co integrating rank r.

The idea behind the parametric bootstrap is to approximate the finite sample distribution of the $L\hat{R}$, $\hat{W}$, $\hat{F}$ type test by drawing several B bootstrap realizations $\{L\hat{R}_i^*\},\{\hat{W}_i^*\}$ or $\{\hat{F}_i^*\}$ for i =1....B bootstrap samples $\{(\Delta Y^*, Y_{t-1}^*)_i\}$. In order to do this the residuals $(\varepsilon_1 .... \varepsilon_t)$ are re-sampled from (5.22) and a bootstrap sample $(\varepsilon_1^* .... \varepsilon_t^*)$ is obtained. The bootstrap algorithm can be summarized as follows:

1. Estimate the error correction model given by (5.22) and compute $L\hat{R}, \hat{W}$ and $\hat{F}$.

2. Resample the residuals from $(\hat{\varepsilon}_1 .... \hat{\varepsilon}_t)$ with replacements to obtain a bootstrap sample $(\varepsilon_1^* .... \varepsilon_t^*)$. Generate the bootstrap sample $Y_1^* .... Y_t^*$ recursively from $Y_0 = 0$ and $(\varepsilon_1^* .... \varepsilon_t^*)$ using the estimated restricted model

$$\Delta Y_t = \tilde{\gamma} \, \tilde{\beta}' Y_{t-1} + \hat{\alpha} + \varepsilon_t^*$$

Where $\tilde{\gamma}$ and $\tilde{\beta}$ denote the restricted estimates under the null $\beta = H\Psi$.

3. Compute the bootstrap replication of $\{L\hat{R}^*\}$, $\{\hat{W}^*\}$ or $\{\hat{F}^*\}$ using $\{Y_1^* ...... Y_t^*\}$.

4. Repeat steps 2 to 4 B times. Defining the bootstrap p values function by the quantity

$$p^*(\hat{\theta}) = \frac{\sum_{i=1}^{B} I(\theta^* \geq \hat{\theta})}{B} \quad \text{.......} \quad (5.23)$$

Where $\hat{\theta}$ is the test statistic considered and I { } is the indicator function that equals 1 if the inequality is satisfied and zero otherwise.

5. Reject the null hypothesis if the selected significance level exceeds $p^*[\hat{\theta}]$.

Thus, the distribution of $\sqrt{T}(\hat{\theta}-\theta)$ can be approximated by the bootstrap distribution of $\sqrt{T}(\hat{\theta}^*-\theta)$. Asymptotic validity of the bootstrap requires that with probability 1 the asymptotic distribution of $\sqrt{T}$ $(\hat{\theta}^*-\theta)$ conditional on $\{F_t: t \geq 1\}$ equals the distribution of $\sqrt{T}$ $(\hat{\theta}-\theta)$.

The study suggested that in case of uncertainty about the co-integrating rank, tests on β should be conducted under different assumptions about r. If the conclusions changed with an increase in r, especially if the bootstrap test results start to diverge from those of asymptotic tests, then only the results for smaller r should be relied upon.

Following Engle (1982), ARCH-GARCH models have been extensively used in financial literature to capture volatility clustering in financial returns. Lamoureux and Lastrapes (1990) proposed the use of recursive bootstrap in the generalized autoregressive conditional heteroskedasticity (GARCH) models. They considered the following GARCH (1,1) model

$$Y_t = \alpha.Y_{t-1} + \varepsilon_t \text{ .... (5.24)}$$

$$h_t = \gamma + \theta\varepsilon_{t-1}^2 + \lambda.h_{t-1} \text{ .... (5.25)}$$

Where $\varepsilon_t \sim f(0, h_t)$ with any distribution f.

They first estimated the GARCH model (5.24) and (5.25) to get $\hat{\varepsilon}$ and $\hat{h}$. Then $\hat{\varepsilon}\sqrt{\hat{h}}$ is resampled with replacement to create the bootstrap errors. The bootstrap samples h* and Y* are recursively computed with ε_0 and Y_0 specified to be 0 and h_0 to be the unconditional variance of ε. These steps are repeated to compute the bootstrap estimates of the parameters.

Various bootstrap methods for multivariate regression model have been proposed in the literature. For example Chou (2001) Hein, Westfall and Zhang (HWZ) (2001) bootstrap the raw data to estimate the distribution of test statistics and such methods are called "data based bootstrap methods". Kramer (2001) bootstrapped the test statistics themselves to estimate their distribution and this method is called "test statistic-based bootstrap method".

These two types of bootstrap work well in the absence of cross-sectional correlation, even though the data may exhibit time series dependencies such as AR, ARCH and GARCH effects. However, the test statistic based bootstrap procedure results in grossly inflated type I error rates in the presence of cross-sectional correlation. Therefore test-statistic based bootstrap methods are recommended for event studies with multiple events at independent time points and for the same reason should not be used for clustered event studies. Moreover the test statistic based bootstrap not only offers flexibility to accommodate cross-sectional correlation but also the ability to test for events when there are a small number of firms.

On the other hand, the Kramer procedure of summing t statistics has potentially more power than HWZ procedure. Another alternative method as proposed by Hein and Westfall (2004) involves the use of summed t statistic in conjunction with the data based bootstrap. This new method is claimed to have both good power and control of type I error rates under the presence of cross-sectional correlation as well as under the time series dependence structures.

Karolyi and Kho (1994) working in a multivariate framework used bootstrap methods and trading rules for the purpose of checking the adequacy of several commonly used models like random walk model with drift and Fama and French multifactor models with and without conditioning instrumental variables, with and without auto correlated, cross-auto correlated and conditionally heteroskedastic errors using resampling techniques both with and without replacement.

The authors used an estimation based bootstrap simulations procedure to assess the ability of different models. In this method each model was fitted to the original series to obtain parameters and residuals. The residuals were then standardized using estimated standard deviation for the error process. The estimated residuals were then sampled to form scrambled residual series which was then used with the estimated parameters to form a new representative series for the given null model. Each of the simulations was based on 500 replications of the null model which was estimated separately for each of the sample stock.

The study results revealed that for the random walk-model, the bootstrap simulations with replacement was unable to yield momentum spreads as large as in the real data. Modeling with time-varying expected returns using lagged information variables improved the predictive power, but not enough to capture the total momentum returns. Also simulations using a sampling procedure without replacements obtained much weaker results even with the use of information variables.

Others including LeBaron (1991), Brock et al. (1992), Kim (1994) used bootstrap methods to evaluate asset models. All the above papers agreed with Karolyi and Kho in rejecting the random walk model. The trading rules considered in Brock et al (1992), LeBaron (1991) and Kim (1994) are moving average rules and those considered by Karolyi and Kho are the positive feedback investment rules. In all the cases the bootstrap method in conjunction with the trading rules has been used as a tool for model specification.

5.6.2 Heteroskedastic Errors

In this case the bootstrap samples must be generated in such a way that the relationship between the variance of each error terms and the corresponding regressors is retained. The simplest way to deal with heteroskedasticity, which was originally proposed by Freedman (1981) is called bootstrapping pairs or the pair bootstrap. Consider the linear regression model

$$Y_t = \beta.X_t + \varepsilon_t, \varepsilon_t = \sigma_t v_t, E(v_t) = 1 \ \text{.......} \ (5.26)$$

where, σ_t^2, the variance of the error terms depends on the regressors in an unknown fashion. The idea of bootstrapping pairs is to resample the regressand and the regressors together. Thus, the tth row of each bootstrap regressor is

$$Y_t^* = \beta.X_t^* + \varepsilon_t \ \text{.......} \ (5.27)$$

where the row vector $[Y_t^* \ X_t^*]$ is equal to each of the row vector $[Y_s \ X_s]$ for s = 1 with probability 1/n.

Thus, a parametric bootstrap DGP is not specified here. Instead the bootstrap data are generated from the empirical distribution function of the real data. Since the regressor matrix will be different for each of the bootstrap samples, the pairs bootstrap does not make sense if the regressors are thought of as fixed in repeated samples.

When using the pairs bootstrap one cannot impose a parametric null hypothesis on β. In order to compute a bootstrap p value one needs to change the null hypothesis to the one that is compatible with the data. If the hypothesis of interest is that β_1 equals some specified value then one needs to compare the actual statistic for testing this hypothesis that $\beta_1 = \bar{\beta}_1$. Bootstrap p values are then compared in the usual way.

An alternative way to deal with heteroskedasticity is to use what is called the wild bootstrap which was proposed by Liu (1988) and further developed by Mammen (1993). Once again consider the model $Y_i^* = \beta.X_i^* + \varepsilon_i^*$. For testing restrictions on this model, the wild bootstrap DGP would be

$$Y_t = \hat{\beta}.X_t + f(\hat{\varepsilon}_t)v_t \ \ldots\ldots (5.28)$$

Where $\hat{\beta}$ denotes the OLS estimates subject to the restrictions that is being tested, $f(\hat{\varepsilon}_t)$ is a transformation of the tth residual $\hat{\varepsilon}_t$ associated with $\hat{\beta}$ and v is a random variable with mean zero and variance one.

One possible choice for the function f(.) is

$$f(\hat{\varepsilon}_t) = \frac{\hat{\varepsilon}_t}{\sqrt{(1 - h_t)}}$$

which ensures that the $f(\hat{\varepsilon}_t)$ would have constant variance if the error terms are homoskedastic. There are in principle many ways to specify the random variable v_t. By far the most popular is the two-point distribution

$$F_1 : v_t = \begin{cases} \dfrac{-(\sqrt{5} - 1)}{2} with.probability \ (\sqrt{5} + 1) \Big/ 2\sqrt{5} \\[2em] \dfrac{(\sqrt{5} + 1)}{2} with.probability \ (\sqrt{5} - 1) \Big/ 2\sqrt{5} \end{cases}$$

This distribution was suggested by Mammen (1993). A much simpler two-point distribution called Rademacher distributions is

$F_2 : v_t = $ -1 with probability 1/2

$\qquad\quad$ +1 with probability 1/2

Davidson and Flachaire (2001) have recently shown on the basis of both theoretical analysis and simulation experiments that wild bootstrap tests based on

Rademacher distribution F_2 will usually perform better in finite samples than one based on F_1.

In some respects the error terms for wild bootstrap DGP do not resemble those of the true DGP at all. When a two point distribution is used the bootstrap error term can take only two possible values for each observation. With F_2 these are just plus and minus $F(\hat{\varepsilon}_t)$. Nevertheless the wild bootstrap does mimic the essential features of the true DGP well enough for it to be useful in many cases.

5.6.3 Simultaneous equations models

Here again the standard bootstrap does not work perfectly. Bootstrapping even one equation of a simultaneous equations model is a good deal more complicated than bootstrapping an equation in which all the explanatory variables are exogenous or predetermined. The problem is that the bootstrap DGP must provide a way to generate all the endogenous variables not just one of them.

The class of models for which 2SLS is appropriate can be written as

$$Y = Z\gamma + X_1\beta + \varepsilon$$

$$Z = X\pi + v \quad \text{.......(5.29)}$$

where Y is a vector of observations on an endogenous variable of particular interest, Z is a matrix of observations on other exogenous variables, X is a matrix of observations on exogenous or predetermined variables and X_1 consists of some of the columns of X.

The first equation of (5.29) can be estimated consistently by 2SLS, but 2SLS estimates are usually biased in finite samples. They can be seriously misleading even when the sample size is large if some of the reduced form of equation for z has little explanatory power.

In order to bootstrap the 2SLS estimates of β and γ one needs to generate bootstrap samples containing both Y* and Z*. For a semi-parametric bootstrap one needs estimates of β, γ and π. These would normally be 2SLS estimates of the parameters of the first (structural) equation and OLS estimates of the parameters of the remaining (reduced) form of equations. One can then obtain the bootstrap error terms by resampling rows of residual matrix $[\hat{\varepsilon}, \hat{v}]$, maybe after rescaling. Alternatively, one could assume normality and use a fully parametric bootstrap.

A simpler approach which also allows for hetereoskedasticity is to use the pairs bootstrap; this was proposed by Freedman and Peters (1984). However as already noted this approach is less than ideal for testing hypothesis and it can be expected to work even less than the semi-parametric approach when the error terms are homoskedasitc.

The finite sample distribution of the 2SLS estimates are quite sensitive to some of the parameters that appear in the bootstrap DGP.

Thus, the bootstrap is a very useful tool in improving the finite sample performance of the statistic under consideration. Although bootstrapping may work well in some cases it would be unrealistic to expect it to work all the time.

5.7 BOOTSTRAP APPROACH TO ESTIMATION OF BEHAVIORAL INERTIA MODEL

In general the presence of lagged dependent variable implies that the OLS does not give an unbiased estimation. Specifically, the coefficient for the lagged dependent variable is upwardly biased and estimates of the connection between exogenous explanatory factors and the dependent variable are biased downward and coefficients for other explanatory factors are attenuated towards zero. With biased parameter estimates hypothesis testing will only be approximately valid.

However, it can be established that if the error processes is serially uncorrelated then the lagged dependent variable will be uncorrelated with the current period error and the OLS estimator will be consistent in large samples. Since the model under consideration does not exhibit any serial correlation, the parameter estimates can be treated as consistent.

In the OLS exercise for estimating the behavioral inertia model we undertook two large sample test- the LM test for detecting serial correlation and the wald test for the test of inertia. In small samples these asymptotic tests may have size distortions and therefore actual levels of significance have to be established for a correct test of the null hypothesis. Many Monte-Carlo studies have found that the use of asymptotic χ^2 distribution leads to misleading inferences. The bootstrap method can be used to get more accurate small sample inferences.

In the bootstrap framework there are two approaches for drawing inferences about the population parameters, one based on the confidence interval and the other the simulation based estimation of p values. The latter requires drawing a sample of the statistic of interest from the empirical distribution under the restrictions specified by the null. And then the achieved significance level or p values can be obtained by finding the proportion of bootstrap statistic that are more extreme than the obtained from the sample under consideration.

The bootstrap approach for testing a hypothesis involves estimating the model under the constraints given by the null hypothesis. Thus, for example for the test of hypothesis $\beta = \beta_0$, the model under consideration (say

$$Y_t = \beta X_t + u_t \ldots\ldots\ldots(5.30))$$ is estimated by putting $\beta = \beta_0$, and the

residuals $\tilde{u}_t = Y_t - \beta_0 X_t$ are generated. This $\tilde{u}_t$ vector of residuals forms the bootstrap DGP from which resampled vectors are drawn with replacement. The reason for estimating the model under the null is that if the null of $\beta = \beta_0$ is true, but the OLS estimator $\hat{\beta}$ gives a value of β far away from β_0, the empirical distribution of the residuals will suffer from a poor approximation of the distribution of errors under the null.

The bootstrap samples of residuals are next plugged back in the model and Y*(bootstrap samples of Y) are generated using β_0 (i.e. null hypothesis parameter values).

Thus, $$Y_t^* = \beta_0 X_t + u_t^* \ldots\ldots\ldots\ldots\ldots\ldots\ldots\ldots\ldots\ldots\ldots\ldots(5.31)$$

Alternatively, the model can be first estimated by OLS and the OLS residuals generated. Bootstrap samples of residuals from this vector of OLS residuals can then be drawn. Using these bootstrap samples of residuals and $\hat{\beta}$ we can then generate Y*. This would correspond to an unrestricted estimation of the model. Another possible sampling scheme for Y* would involve the use of OLS residuals and β_0.

Thus, in the literature three sampling schemes have been used:

$$S1: \quad Y_t^* = \beta_0 X_t^* + u_{0t}$$

$$S2: \quad Y_t^* = \hat{\beta} X_t^* + u_t^*$$

$$S3: \quad Y_t^* = \beta_0 X_t^* + u_t^* \quad \dots\dots\dots\dots\dots\dots\dots\dots\dots\dots\dots\dots(5.32).$$

Where u* is the resampled residuals obtained by resampling the OLS residuals and u_{0t}^* is the residuals obtained by resampling $\tilde{u}_t = Y_t - \beta_0 X_t$. The literature also reports two different ways of defining test statistics. These are

$$T_1 : T(\hat{\beta}) = (\hat{\beta}^* - \hat{\beta}) / \hat{\sigma}^*$$

$$T_2 : T(\beta_0) = (\hat{\beta}^* - \beta_0) / \hat{\sigma}^*$$

where $\hat{\sigma}^*$ is the estimate of σ from the bootstrap sample. The test statistic T_1 is appropriate for sampling scheme S_2 and the statistic T_2 is best suited for sampling schemes S_1 and S_3.

5.7.1 Bootstrapping the Breusch-Godfrey serial correlation test

Mantalos (2003) had pointed out that when the autocorrelation of price change is small but persistently positive (or negative) standard test for significance of autocorrelation are unlikely to reject null of serial correlation. Despite the presence of lagged dependent variables the Breusch-Godfrey test reported in the chapter 4 does not support the presence of serial correlation in any of the sample companies. To verify the absence of serial correlation we redid the Breusch-Godfrey test using the technique of bootstrap.

The Breusch-Godfey test is a general test for serial correlation valid for both autoregressive and moving average errors. This test is derived from the Lagrange multiplier principle. Consider the regression model

$$Y_t = \alpha_0 + \alpha_1 Y_{t-1} + \alpha_2 Y_{t-2} + \beta_1 X_{1t} + \beta_2 X_{2t} + \cdots \beta_k X_{kt} + u_t \cdots t = 1 - T$$

$$\cdots\cdots\cdots\cdots\cdots (5.33)$$

and

$$u_t = \rho_1 u_{t-1} + \rho_2 u_{t-2} + \cdots \rho_{1p} u_{t-p} + e_t$$

$$e_t \sim IN(0, \sigma^2) \cdots\cdots\cdots\cdots\cdots (5.34)$$

The null hypothesis to be tested is

$$H_0 : \rho_1 = \rho_2 \cdots \rho_p = 0$$

The Breusch-Godfrey test involves estimating equation (5.33) by OLS and obtaining the least squares residuals $\hat{u}_t$. Next the following regression equation is estimated

$$\hat{\mu}_t = \alpha_0 + \alpha_1 Y_{t-1} + \alpha_2 Y_{t-2} + \beta_1 X_{t-1} + \cdots \beta_k X_{t-k} + \sum_{i=1}^{p} \hat{u}_{t-i} \rho_i + \eta_t$$

$$\cdots\cdots\cdots\cdots\cdots (5.35)$$

and a test of the coefficient of all the $\hat{u}_{t-i}$ being equal to zero is undertaken. The calculated F and the number of restrictions p gives us a χ^2 variable with d.f. p.

An alternative estimation procedure involves estimating the OLS coefficients for (5.33) and getting the residuals and again estimate the following model by OLS.

$$Y_t = \alpha_0 + \alpha_1 Y_{t-1} + \alpha_2 Y_{t-2} + \beta_1 X_{t-1} + \cdots \beta_k X_{t-k} + \sum_{i=1}^{p} \hat{u}_{t-i} \rho_i + \eta_t$$

$$\cdots\cdots\cdots\cdots\cdots (5.36)$$

The F statistic for testing the null hypothesis is again computed as $\rho F \sim \chi^2$ with ρ degrees of freedom and inference is drawn.

For bootstrapping the test for serial correlation we use the recursive bootstrap approach. Since our model involves lagged dependent variables we generated bootstrap sample of Y* in a recursive manner so as to preserve the time dependency of the Y series. This approach involves the following steps.

1. Estimate the model under the null of no serial correlation by regressing $\ln P_t$ on $\ln P_{t-1}$, $\ln P_{t-2}$, lnB/M, lnMV, lnbeta and lnbeta negative.

2. Obtain the OLS residuals u_t. From this residual vector through random resampling with replacement we generate a bootstrap sample vector of residuals.

3. Using the first element of the resampled residual vector along with the OLS coefficients of $\ln P_{t-1}$, $\ln P_{t-2}$, lnB/M, lnMV, lnbeta and lnbeta negative obtained in step 1, and the first row of the following matrix of explanatory variables we generate $\ln P_1{}^*$.

$$\begin{bmatrix} 1 & \ln P_0 & \ln P_{-1} & \ln B/M_1 & \ln MV_1 & \ln \text{beta}_1 & \ln \text{betaneg}_1 \\ 1 & \ln P_1 & \ln P_0 & \ln B/M_2 & \ln MV_2 & \ln \text{beta}_2 & \ln \text{betaneg}_2 \\ 1 & \ln P_2 & \ln P_1 & \ln B/M_3 & \ln MV_3 & \ln \text{beta}_3 & \ln \text{betaneg}_3 \\ .. & ...... & .... & .... & .... & .... & .... \\ 1 & \ln P_{64} & \ln P_{63} & \ln B/M_{65} & \ln MV_1 & \ln \text{beta}_{65} & \ln \text{betaneg}_{65} \\ 1 & \ln P_{65} & \ln P_{64} & \ln B/M_{66} & \ln MV_{66} & \ln \text{beta}_{66} & \ln \text{betaneg}_{66} \end{bmatrix}$$

$$\dots\dots\dots\dots\dots\dots\dots\dots\dots\dots\dots\dots\dots\dots\dots\dots\dots(5.37)$$

Thus,

$$\ln P_1^* = \hat{\beta}_0 + \hat{\beta}_1 \ln P_0 + \hat{\beta}_2 \ln P_{-1} + \hat{\beta}_3 \ln \frac{B}{M_1} + \hat{\beta}_4 \ln MV_1 +$$

$$\hat{\beta}_5 \ln \text{beta}_1 + \hat{\beta}_6 \ln \text{betaneg}_1 + \mu 1_1^*$$

$$\dots\dots\dots\dots\dots\dots\dots\dots\dots(5.38)$$

where $\hat{\beta}_0$, $\hat{\beta}_1$, $\hat{\beta}_2$, $\hat{\beta}_3$ $\hat{\beta}_4$, $\hat{\beta}_5$, $\hat{\beta}_6$ are the OLS estimates and $\mu 1_1^*$ the first element of the bootstrap resample residual vector.

4. For generating the second element of lnP_t^* we use the second element of the bootstrap sample residual vector along with the second row of the matrix of explanatory variables and OLS estimates but with lnP_1^* replacing lnP_1.

5. The third and subsequent elements of lnP_t^* are generated similarly but with lnP_{t-1}^* and lnP_{t-2}^* replacing lnP_{t-1} and lnP_{t-2}.

The new vector of lnP_t^* is therefore given as

$$
\begin{bmatrix} \ln P_1^* \\ \ln P_2^* \\ \ln P_3^* \\ .... \\ \ln P_{65}^* \\ \ln P_{66}^* \end{bmatrix} = \begin{bmatrix} 1 & \ln P_0 & \ln P_{-1} & \ln B/M_1 & \ln MV_1 & \ln beta_1 & \ln betaneg_1 \\ 1 & \ln P_1^* & \ln P_0 & \ln B/M_2 & \ln MV_2 & \ln beta_2 & \ln betaneg_2 \\ 1 & \ln P_2^* & \ln P_1^* & \ln B/M_3 & \ln MV_3 & \ln beta_3 & \ln betaneg_3 \\ .. & .... & .... & .... & .... & .... & .... \\ 1 & \ln P_{64}^* & \ln P_{63}^* & \ln B/M_{65} & \ln MV_1 & \ln beta_{65} & \ln betaneg_{65} \\ 1 & \ln P_{65}^* & \ln P_{64}^* & \ln B/M_{66} & \ln MV_{66} & \ln beta_{66} & \ln betaneg_{66} \end{bmatrix} \cdot \begin{bmatrix} \hat{\beta}_0 \\ \hat{\beta}_1 \\ \hat{\beta}_2 \\ \hat{\beta}_3 \\ \hat{\beta}_4 \\ \hat{\beta}_5 \\ \hat{\beta}_6 \end{bmatrix} + \begin{bmatrix} \mu 1_1^* \\ \mu 1_2^* \\ \mu 1_3^* \\ .... \\ \mu 1_{65}^* \\ \mu 1_{66}^* \end{bmatrix}
$$

$$............(5.39)$$

6. In the next step the newly generated lnP_t^* vector is regressed on the matrix of explanatory variables given in (5.37) but with lnP_1 and the subsequent lnP_t's being replaced by the generated values and the lagged residuals. Thus the new vector of coefficients is estimated using the following matrix of explanatory variables.

$$
\begin{bmatrix} 1 & \ln P_0 & \ln P_{-1} & \ln B/M_1 & \ln MV_1 & \ln beta_1 & \ln betaneg_1 & \mu 1_0^* & \mu 1_{-1}^* \\ 1 & \ln P_1^* & \ln P_0 & \ln B/M_2 & \ln MV_2 & \ln beta_2 & \ln betaneg_2 & \mu 1_1^* & \mu 1_0^* \\ 1 & \ln P_2^* & \ln P_1^* & \ln B/M_3 & \ln MV_3 & \ln beta_3 & \ln betaneg_3 & \mu 1_2^* & \mu 1_1^* \\ .. & ...... & .... & .... & .... & .... & .... & .... & .... \\ 1 & \ln P_{64}^* & \ln P_{63}^* & \ln B/M_{65} & \ln MV_1 & \ln beta_{65} & \ln betaneg_{65} & \mu 1_{64}^* & \mu 1_{63}^* \\ 1 & \ln P_{65}^* & \ln P_{64}^* & \ln B/M_{66} & \ln MV_{66} & \ln beta_{66} & \ln betaneg_{66} & \mu 1_{65}^* & \mu 1_{64}^* \end{bmatrix}
$$

$$............(5.40)$$

7. The test of no serial correlation is done by running the F test and generating a χ^2 statistic as equal to 2xF (here 2 is the number of restrictions)

8. We repeat steps 2-7 one thousand times to generate one thousand resampled residual vector and corresponding one thousand $\ln P_t^*$ vectors and χ^2 statistic.

10. The P value of the Breusch-Godfrey test is obtained by finding the proportion of samples whose χ^2 statistic exceeds the χ^2 value of the original sample.

The p values associated with the bootstrapping of Breusch-Godfrey test is given in Table 5.1.

Table 5.1. p values of the Breusch-Godfrey test.

COMPANY NAME	p Value
ACE	0.431
AFTE	0.548
BLUESTAR	0.164
CMC	0.823
COSMO	0.868
CREST	0.510
CYBERSYS	0.193
DSQ	0.655
ESERVE	0.298
FINOLEX	0.189
HCL	0.346
HINDUJA	0.283
INFOSYS	0.779
JAIN	0.734
MASTEK	0.266
MOSER	0.539
MPHASIS	0.219
MTNL	0.756
NIIT	0.129
ORIENT	0.574
PENTAMEDIA	0.797
PENTASOFT	0.382
SATYAM	0.519
TATA ELXSI	0.044
TRIGYN	0.270
VINDHYA	0.737
VISUALSOFT	0.369
VSNL	0.241
WIPRO	0.017
ZEE	0.185
ZENITH	0.966
ZENSAR	0.028

The bootstrap results again strongly support the absence of serial correlation in residuals. Only three companies namely TataElxsi, Wipro and Zensar fail to accept the absence of serial correlation at 5 % level of significance. All the sample companies, however, accept the null at 1 % level of significance.

5.7.2 Bootstrapping the wald test

A similar exercise was done for bootstrapping the wald test, the steps for which are noted below.

1. The first step in the bootstrap exercise is to estimate the model under the null. Writing the set of restrictions $\beta1 + \beta2 = 1$ in the form $Rb = R$ we get

$$R = \begin{bmatrix} 0 & 1 & 1 & 0 & 0 & 0 & 0 \end{bmatrix}$$
$$b^{T} = \begin{bmatrix} \beta_0 & \beta_1 & \beta_2 & \beta_3 & \beta_4 & \beta_5 & \beta_6 \end{bmatrix}$$
$$and$$
$$r = 1$$

A solution to the behavioral model under the null hypothesis restriction is possible as the number of rows of R is smaller than the number of columns of the R. Thus regressing $\ln P_t$ on $\ln P_{t-1}$, $\ln P_{t-2}$, lnB/M, lnMV, lnbeta and lnbeta negative under the null hypothesis restriction we get restricted least square estimates. The vector of RLS coefficient estimates can also be obtained by using the relation

$$b_{RLS} = b_{OLS} + (X'X)^{-1} R' [R(X'X)^{-1}R']^{-1} (r-Rb).$$

Here X denotes the matrix of explanatory variables as given in (5.37)

2. Using the $\hat{b}_{RLS}$ coefficients and the $\ln P_t$ vector we next find $\hat{u}_{RLS}$, i.e. residuals of the restricted least square.

3. Now through random resampling with replacement we pick a vector containing sixty six elements from the restricted residuals set.

4. Using the first element of the bootstrap sample of residual and the first row of the matrix of explanatory variables given in (5.37) and $\hat{b}_{RLS}$ coefficients we estimate lnP1*.

5. We next pick the element in the second row from the sampled vector of residuals and using the second row of the matrix of explanatory variables but with lnP_1* replacing lnP_1 and the $\hat{b}_{RLS}$ coefficient vector we generate lnP_2*.

6. For lnP_3* we pick the third element in the $\hat{u}_{RLS}$ and using the third row of matrix of explanatory variables with lnP_1* and lnP_2* substituted for lnP_1 and lnP_2 and the $\hat{b}_{RLS}$ vector we estimate lnP_3*.

7. Subsequent elements of lnP_t* are generated in a similar fashion by using lnP_{t-1}* and lnP_{t-2}*

8. Now, using the generated vector of lnPt* and the new matrix of explanatory variables i.e the regressor and the regressand given in (5.39) we re-estimate the model by OLS.

9. The wald test for the sum of the regression coefficients of the two lagged price variables adding up to one is undertaken for this new model and the χ^2 value noted.

10. Steps 3 to 9 is repeated thousand times to generate thousand vectors of bootstrap sample of residuals, thousand vectors of generated lnPt* and thousand χ^2 statistic.

11. Finally the P value of the wald test is obtained by finding the proportion of bootstrap samples whose χ^2 statistic exceeds the χ^2 value of the original sample.

The software program formulated for the above exercise is given in Appendix A6. The results of the above exercise are given in Table 5.2.

Table 5.2. p values of the wald test.

COMPANY NAME	p Value
ACE	0.130
AFTE	0.063
BLUESTAR	0.211
CMC	0.053
COSMO	0.193
CREST	0.057
CYBERSYS	0.659
DSQ	0.060
ESERVE	0.232
FINOLEX	0.196
HCL	0.070
HINDUJA	0.638
INFOSYS	0.032
JAIN	0.247
MASTEK	0.434
MOSER	0.211
MPHASIS	0.007
MTNL	0.207
NIIT	0.004
ORIENT	0.070
PENTAMEDIA	0.111
PENTASOFT	0.022
SATYAM	0.011
TATA ELXSI	0.267
TRIGYN	0.075
VINDHYA	0.362
VISUALSOFT	0.071
VSNL	0.027
WIPRO	0.232
ZEE	0.045
ZENITH	0.012
ZENSAR	0.223

From the Table 5.2 it is clear that the model now rejects the null for only two out of the thirty-two sample companies, evaluated at 1% level of significance. These two companies are namely Mphasis and NIIT. Evaluated at 5% the null is not accepted for a total of eight companies. These include Infosys, Mphasis and NIIT, Pentasoft, Satyam, VSNL, Zee, and Zenith.

5.8 CONCLUSIONS

Bootstrapping asymptotically pivotal statistics such as wald statistics yields asymptotic improvements compared to the standard least squares formulas. Asymptotic χ^2 distributed tests like wald tests are quite heavily affected by the sample size. By bootstrapping we replicate any skewness in the finite sample distribution and hence the bootstrap distribution of wald statistic can account for deviations of the actual distribution from the asymptotic distribution. Bootstrap thus enables us to approximate the finite sample distribution of wald statistic and therefore more reliable inferences can be drawn. The rejection of the null hypothesis of presence of inertia in a smaller number of companies with the bootstrap approach as compared to the number rejected in the OLS framework leads us to strongly support our hypothesis of presence of inertia in the stock market during the study period.

CHAPTER 6: SUMMARY AND CONCLUSIONS

The focus of this study has been on developing a behavioral model for understanding asset market behavior. Popular stock investment strategies are often fads based on market generated data, especially share price as opposed to accounting data given in the company financial reports. Agents assume the current market valuation to be a reflection of the markets assessment of future prospects. Acting on the belief that prices will be what they were, investors use market valuation to pick stocks. Such behavior is self fulfilling and inertia becomes the basis for the market action.

This behavioral pattern is captured by the use of lagged price variables in our model. Further, by identifying factors that influence market valuation, we infuse dynamism into the model. Professional financial analysts too spend considerable resources in trying to predict both changes in fundamentals and also possible changes in the sentiment of other investors. The focus on lagged price variables is the distinctive feature of our behavior model.

The behavioral inertia approach involves the use of a simple regression exercise. Complex econometric techniques though highly popular generally do not serve much purpose. When using any of the more advanced estimation procedure the researcher can never be sure whether the complication treated by the chosen technique is an incidental manifestation of deeper misspecification or not. By assuming inertial decay we derive a log-linear model to describe stock price behavior. The model's specification is guided by theory rather than an outcome of sample data. Since no inductive searches for suitable econometric models are made, there is no pre-test bias. Any problem in empirical testing either in the form of misspecified error terms or coefficients with wrong sign is treated as evidence against the theory under examination. This is in contrast to the usual approach of modifying a model to arrive a better fit to the data in hand. This latter approach is not a desirable method of model building as corrections made by looking at apparent deviations from the assumptions may or may not eliminate the root cause of the problem.

In the behavioral inertia approach no distribution assumptions are made about the error term except them being identically and independently distributed. Further, by including caprice or random behavior we explicitly incorporate error term into theory.

In the financial literature most studies use stock beta and accounting variables to model stock prices. A model that is often used as a benchmark in studying returns behavior is the Fama and French (1993) three-factor model. To begin with, we undertook an empirical estimation of the Fama and French model using the sample data set. In this model three-factor portfolios accounting for beta, book-to-market value and size are used to explain cross-sectional variation in average returns. A simple univariate regression exercise at the stock level showed poor performance of all the variables. The multifactor model also did not bring about any appreciable improvement in the result. In the Fama and French model high book-to-market value firms and small size firms are treated as more risky than low book-to-market value firms and large sized firms. The risk associated with high book-to-market value firms gets priced and is reflected in higher returns and positive coefficient on the HML factor portfolio (h_i) as against low book-to-market firms which will have negative loadings on h_i. Similarly, small firms will have higher expected returns and positive slope on SMB as against big firms which have lower expected returns and negative slope on SMB.

The Fama and French model is tested using portfolios constructed on the basis of BE/ME and EPS/P ranking. The results show poor performance of the model in explaining average returns on the various constructed portfolios. In particular in the BE/ME ranking the null hypothesis of the three-factor portfolios being minimum variance efficient is accepted only for the six size-BE/ME equal weighted portfolios, and the small and medium BE/ME value weighted portfolios. A similar number of portfolios in the EPS/P ranking also accept the null hypothesis. These are low EPS (both equal and value weighted), small and medium EPS (both equal and value weighted), big and low EPS (both equal and value weighted), small and low EPS value weighted portfolios.

The coefficients on SMB and HML also do not unambiguously reflect the pricing of risk associated with small size and high book-to-market value firms.

A multivariate joint test of all categories of portfolios falling in particular ranking criteria with similar portfolio weights using the test statistic developed by Gibbons et al. (1989) fails to reject the null hypothesis that the market prices risk associated with small size and high book-to-market value firms. The result of this test however, has to be interpreted carefully as the outcome of the test is sensitive to the number of portfolios as well as the choice of asset sets.

In the chapter on behavioral principles in stock market we undertook an empirical validation of our model. The presence of inertia in the stock price series is ascertained by undertaking a 't' test on the coefficients of the two lagged variables adding up to 1. Under the condition when no distributional assumptions are made about the returns series, an asymptotic test like wald test would be more appropriate. We, therefore, undertook a wald test of the null hypothesis of presence of inertia. The results of both the 't' test and 'wald' test show that the null is not accepted in 10 out of 32 sample companies, namely, Bluestar, Finolex, Jain, Mphasis, MTNL, NIIT, Satyam, TataElxsi, Wipro and Zensar.

An in-sample forecasting of the two models viz. Fama and French and the behavioral inertia model, formulated using rational and behavioral approaches respectively, also supported our argument for incorporating behavioral biases in investor's behavior.

The OLS exercise gave us consistent estimates, but had poor small sample properties. The estimates are biased because of the inclusions of lagged-dependent variables and the presence of error in the measurement of beta variable. Specifically, the coefficients for the lagged dependent variable are upwardly biased. The presence of error in the measurement of the variables lnbeta and lnbeta neg causes biases in not only the coefficients of these variables but also in the coefficients of $\ln P_{t-1}$ and $\ln P_{t-2}$. The direction of the bias can be ascertained only after looking at the value of the coefficients of lnbeta, lnbeta neg, and the covariance between the explanatory variables. Thus, a priori, the direction of the bias cannot be inferred and hence the reliability of the test statistics cannot be established. Further, the wald test is an asymptotic test and suffers from size distortion in finite samples.

In order to overcome the above limitation, we employed the bootstrap test (Chapter 5) to evaluate our model. The Breusch- Godfrey serial correlation test that we undertook in the OLS framework fails to detect any serial correlation. A bootstrap approach to this test also gave us the same result. Using the technique of recursive bootstrap, we estimated regression of $\ln P_t$ on all the explanatory variables and the lag of residuals. A χ^2 test of the coefficients of the two lag residual terms being equal to zero was undertaken. The result of such a test showed that except for three companies, namely, TataElxsi, Wipro and Zensar, the null hypothesis of no serial correlation was not rejected in any of the other companies at 5% level of significance. At 1% the absence of serial correlation was accepted for all the companies. We next undertook the bootstrap test of behavioral inertia model. Because of the presence of lagged dependent variables we again used the technique of recursive bootstrap and estimated the distribution of the wald test statistic. The p value associated with the test is obtained as the number of bootstrap samples in which wald statistic is greater than the statistic obtained in the original sample. The results of the bootstrap test showed that for only two companies the p values were low enough to reject the null hypothesis of presence of inertia, evaluated at 1% level of significance.

The conclusions of this study, therefore, are:

1. The present study shows bounded rationality of the investors. A behavioral model seems to give a better description of the stock market behavior than a model based on the assumption of perfect rationality

2. For a majority of a sample companies the price movements seems to have been generated by the craze surrounding internet stocks rather than the economic fundamentals of the firms.

3. For the few that did not support the presence of inertia in investor behavior, an examination of the company history revealed that this period was marked by issue of ADRs, major national and international collaborations and high rating of their performance by various agencies. These conveyed information on the future prospects of the firm which were orthogonal to those obtained from the past performance of the firm. The market therefore viewed these stocks favorably and therefore their market prices were driven away from their existing prices.

4. Finally the over-rejection of the null using asymptotic tests seems to suggest the need for bootstrapping the test statistics in small samples. The study also indicates bootstrap as a useful technique for drawing inferences in models with lagged dependent variables and estimated variables.

Thus, the behavioral inertia model developed by us got strong support when evaluated in the bootstrap framework. While the simple linear form of our model does not completely identify nor restrict all potential causes it however provides a dynamic structure that explains how changes in the economic environment affects stock price series.